Margaret M. Johnson's

Festive

FLAVORS  IRELAND

Happy Christmas
Margaret M Johnson

Powerscourt Townhouse, Dublin | *Margaret M. Johnson*

MARGARET M. JOHNSON'S

Festive

FLAVORS  IRELAND

Ambassador International
GREENVILLE, SOUTH CAROLINA & BELFAST, NORTHERN IRELAND

www.ambassador-international.com

Festive Flavors of Ireland

Hardcover ISBN: 978-1-64960-307-4
Paperback ISBN: 978-1-64960-306-7
E-ISBN: 978-1-64960-328-9

Cover photos: (Clockwise, from top left) Peter Goskov; Freeskyline; Kuvona; Jeni Glasgow for *The Garden*, Dublin; Bord Bia, Irish Food Board

Back cover photo: Jessica Guadagno

Cover design by Christopher Aaron
Page layout by Christopher Aaron, Joshua Frederick
Digital Edition by Anna Riebe Raats

AMBASSADOR INTERNATIONAL
Emerald House
411 University Ridge, Suite B14
Greenville, SC 29601, USA
www.ambassador-international.com

AMBASSADOR BOOKS
The Mount
2 Woodstock Link
Belfast, BT6 8DD, Northern Ireland, UK
www.ambassadormedia.co.uk

The colophon is a trademark of Ambassador

The light of the christmas star to you.
the warmth of home and hearth to you.
the cheer and good will of friends to you.
the love of the son and god's peace to you.

Nollaig Shona Buit

happy christmas to you!

The Garden, Dublin | Jeni Glasgow

PRAISE FOR *FESTIVE FLAVORS OF IRELAND*

My first thought after cracking into Margaret M. Johnson's *Festive Flavors of Ireland*—Christmas can't come soon enough! Johnson's latest guide to Irish holiday cuisine, like its predecessor, beckons us to the art and artistry of making delicious meals, while serenading us with the whimsy of Irish culture as we go. Johnson's forte remains crafting meals that anyone can make, but she is also a gifted writer. With seventy Irish holiday recipes on hand, illustrated with world-class photography, indexed and brought to life with her colorful anecdotes, *Festive Flavors of Ireland* offers a passport to Ireland itself.

—GERRY REGAN

Editorial Director, TheWildGeese.irish

It's cliché, I know, but as a card-carrying Irish-American, I immediately jumped to the potato recipes in *Festive Flavors or Ireland*, and when the holidays roll around, Dauphinoise Potatoes will definitely occupy pride of place on my particular groaning board. But of course, there is so much more to Margaret Johnson's newest cookbook, from tasty little palate teasers drawing on Ireland's savory salmon to hearty, meaty mains and sweet, traditional holiday cakes and tarts. It's a thoroughly appetizing and enchanting mélange of Ireland's distinctive cuisine and often curious customs—if you've never heard of Women's Christmas, Margaret is here to inform you! Lavishly illustrated, *Festive Flavors of Ireland* will make your mouth water and instill in you a very merry Christmas spirit.

—JEFF MEADE

Editor, *irishphiladelphia.com*

Open *Festive Flavors of Ireland* and come home to the deliciousness, charm, ancestral wisdom, lore, and feeling in your soul for the magic of the holidays. You'll feel the way Robert Browning did when you delve into this fabulous and lovely cookbook: "God's in His heaven, all's right with the world." Margaret Johnson has created a palette of colorful and scintillating recipes for the palate of all, especially for the Hibernophile.

—CYNTHIA NEALE

Author, *The Irish Dresser* series and *Pavlova in a Hat Box*

Festive Flavors of Ireland is irresistible. Margaret Johnson, with her usual flair, finds a perfect balance between practicality and style, the great traditions and twenty-first century innovation. All of this is heightened by the sense of "great anticipation," to use writer Alice Taylor's term, that accompanies the Irish Christmas from December eighth through January sixth. That and other sprinkles of literary wisdom help set the culinary tone, such as from the poet Alexander Smith, whose line "Christmas is a time that holds all time together" just about sums it up.

—PETER McDERMOTT

Arts Editor, *Irish Echo Newspaper*

TABLE OF CONTENTS

INTRODUCTION

Happy, happy Christmas, that can win us back to the delusions of our childhood days,
recall to the old man the pleasures of his youth,
and transport the traveler back to his own fireside and quiet home!
CHARLES DICKENS, *A Christmas Carol*

Traditionally, the biggest and most important festival in the Christian calendar is Christmas. Nowhere is it greeted more enthusiastically than in Ireland, where the season officially begins on December 8th — a day known as *Mairgead Mór* (Big Fair Day)—and lasts through January 6th—*Nollaig na mBan* (Women's Little Christmas). While the spiritual preparation begins with Advent, four weeks before Christmas, the practical preparations, also known as "getting in the Christmas," begin as early as late October when holiday cakes, puddings, and mincemeat begin to fill pantries and freezers in anticipation of the season.

Alice Taylor, a well-known chronicler of tales of rural Ireland, says Christmas was always the highlight of the year, "a time of great expectations which climaxed with Christmas Eve and Christmas Day, and the Wren Day, which brought a burst of color and music into the quiet countryside." In her book, *The Night Before Christmas*, Taylor says: "The thought of the variety that Christmas would bring filled us with great anticipation. Lemonade, sweet cake, and chocolates in our home at that time were like manna in the desert."

As with holiday traditions throughout the world, food plays a big part. Today, the centerpiece of a traditional menu for Christmas dinner in Ireland is turkey with stuffing and cranberry sauce, although the big bird only first appeared on British tables in the late seventeenth century. By the eighteenth century, wealthy Irish families enjoyed the new delicacy, and it slowly spread to the menu of lower class Irish families as well.

Before the turkey, common fare in poor rural areas was venison, rabbit, goose, and hare. As writer Amhlaoibh Ó Súilleabháin describes in his 1828 diary records: "The poor people [of Kilkenny] are buying pork chops, pigs' heads, big joints of old sows' loins and small bits of old rams." Not so today!

While some contemporary Irish cooks still roast a goose and bake a ham, the traditional side dishes primarily include roasted and mashed potatoes; winter vegetables such as Brussels sprouts, cauliflower, parsnips, and carrots; and treasured sweets such as mincemeat tarts, fruitcake, Christmas pudding and gingerbread. These treats continue to be "must-haves," but it's no surprise that lighter sweets and chocolate desserts also find their way to the laden table.

With more than seventy inspired recipes in five chapters—including easy-to-assemble small bites for holiday parties; appetizing soup and salad starters; tips for preparing the main event; and steamed puddings and fruit-filled trifles—*Festive Flavors of Ireland* offers traditional and trendy holiday dishes made-to-order for the festive season. *Nollaig shona duit!*

CHAPTER ONE

MOREISH MOUTHFULS

SMALL BITES TO CELEBRATE

At Christmas play and make good cheer,
For Christmas comes but once a year.
THOMAS TUSSER, ENGLISH FARMER AND POET

Smoked Salmon on Potato Cakes

Makes 15

HOSTING a holiday party is often the highlight of the season, and you can stress a lot less by serving easy small bites, inspired dips, and tasty spreads. For the festive season, serving Irish smoked salmon is nearly obligatory, and hot- or cold-smoked salmon from premier producers (Burren Smokehouse in Lisdoonvarna, County Clare; Kinvara Smoked Salmon, Kinvara, County Galway; and Ummera in Timoleague, County Cork, to name just a few) is the best way to start. Serve it on these tasty little potato pancakes topped with a dollop of sour cream or crème fraîche. For added decadence, add a bit of red or black caviar.

Potato Cakes

- 2 large potatoes, boiled and mashed (about 1½ cups)
- 1 large egg, beaten
- 2 tablespoons flour
- 1 teaspoon baking powder
- Salt
- Ground black pepper
- ¼ to ½ cup milk
- 1 ounce butter, plus more as needed

- ½ cup sour cream or crème fraîche
- 8 ounces smoked salmon, cut into 24 (½-inch-wide) strips
- Fresh dill, for garnish
- Red or black caviar, for garnish (optional)

1. Make potato cakes. Put potatoes, egg, flour, baking powder, salt, and pepper in a food processor. Pulse 4 to 5 times, or until blended; gradually add enough milk to make a thick batter.
2. In a large skillet over medium-high heat, melt butter. Working in batches, drop spoonsful of potato mixture into pan; cook for 2 to 3 minutes on each side, or until browned. Repeat with additional butter and remaining batter. Serve immediately or cover and refrigerate overnight; reheat in a hot oven.
3. To serve, put a spoonful of sour cream or crème fraîche on top of each pancake. Put a piece of rolled salmon on top and garnish with dill and caviar (if using).

SMOKED SALMON AND AVOCADO PARFAITS

Makes 12

THE flavorful combination of smoked salmon and avocado is highlighted in this impressive appetizer from Graham and Saoirse Roberts, smoked salmon producers at Connemara Smokehouse in picturesque Ballyconneely, County Galway. They suggest serving it in small glass containers known as verrines, but you can make the layers in shot glasses or small Kilner jars.

- 8 ounces cream cheese, at room temperature
- 2 tablespoons chopped fresh flatleaf parsley
- 2 tablespoons minced fresh chives
- 8 ounces smoked salmon, chopped
- 2 avocados
- Juice of 1 lemon
- 1 teaspoon white pepper
- Fresh dill, cilantro or caviar, for garnish
- Bread stick or grissini, for serving

1. In a medium bowl, beat cream cheese, parsley and chives until smooth. Spoon or pipe into twelve 2-ounce glass containers.
2. Divide smoked salmon on top of cream cheese mixture.
3. In a medium bowl, mash avocados. Stir in lemon juice and pepper; spoon over salmon. Garnish with dill, cilantro or caviar. Serve with a bread stick or small spoon.

Beata Aldridge

SAUSAGE ROLLS WITH CRANBERRIES

Makes 36

Sausage rolls are equally at home on a Christmas party plate or as a snack at a hurling match. Here they take on a holiday touch with the addition of cranberry sauce spread alongside the sausage stuffing to create a lovely counterpoint to the spicy meat.

- 2 sheets frozen puff pastry, thawed according to package directions
- 2 pounds pork sausage meat
- ¼ cup plain white breadcrumbs
- 1 tablespoon fresh rosemary
- 1 tablespoon fresh thyme
- Salt
- Ground black pepper
- 1 cup cranberry sauce
- 1 large egg mixed with 1 tablespoon water, for egg wash

1. Preheat oven to 425°F. Line 2 baking sheets with parchment paper.
2. Unfold puff pastry on a lightly floured surface; cut along fold lines of each sheet to create 6 strips.
3. In a large bowl, combine sausage meat, breadcrumbs, rosemary, thyme, salt and pepper. Spread a thin layer of cranberry sauce down center of each strip. With your hands, form sausage mixture into six 1½-inch-thick rolls; place on top of cranberry sauce. Brush sides of each sheet with egg wash; roll to seal.
4. Cut each roll into 6 pieces; place seam-side down on prepared pans. Brush tops with additional egg wash. With tip of a sharp knife, prick 2 to 3 slits in each roll to allow steam to escape.
5. Bake for 15 to 18 minutes, or until rolls are puffed and golden. Serve immediately or at room temperature.

CAMEMBERT TARTLETS WITH PEAR AND APPLE CHUTNEY

Makes 30

FINGER food at its best, tartlets are among the easiest party foods to make, especially when you use prepared filo shells, frozen puff pastry, refrigerated pie dough, and delicious Irish cheese like Cooleeney Camembert—one of a number of artisan cheeses produced at the Maher farmhouse near Thurles, County Tipperary. Top the tartlets with this sweet-tart chutney or Red Onion Marmalade (recipe follows), both of which can be made up to three days ahead.

PEAR AND APPLE CHUTNEY

- 1 small onion, chopped
- ⅓ cup cider vinegar
- 1 teaspoon chopped fresh ginger
- 1 cup (packed) brown sugar
- 4 ounces sultanas (golden raisins)
- 1 small apple, cored and diced
- 1 small pear, cored and diced
- 2 tablespoons chopped walnuts

TARTLETS

- 30 mini phyllo shells, such as Athens brand, or other prepared pastry cups
- 8 ounces camembert cheese, cut into 30 cubes

1. Make pear and apple chutney. In a large saucepan over medium heat, bring onion, vinegar, ginger, sugar, sultanas, apples, and pears to a boil; cook for 2 to 3 minutes. Reduce heat to medium-low and cook, uncovered, for 20 to 25 minutes, or until mixture thickens. Stir in walnuts.
2. Spoon into clean jars; cover and refrigerate for up to 2 weeks. Return to room temperature for serving.
3. Make tartlets. Preheat oven to 350°F. Place phyllo cups on a baking sheet; put 1 cheese cube in each cup.
4. Bake for 5 to 8 minutes, or until cheese is soft. Remove from oven; top each tartlet with a spoonful of chutney. Serve warm or at room temperature.

RED ONION MARMALADE

In a large saucepan over medium heat, melt 1 ounce butter and 2 tablespoons extra virgin olive oil. Add 2 thinly sliced red onions; stir to coat. Stir in ¼ cup (packed) light brown sugar, ½ teaspoon fresh thyme leaves, ½ teaspoon salt, and ½ teaspoon ground black pepper. Reduce heat to medium-low; cook, stirring occasionally, for 25 to 30 minutes, or until onions are soft and caramelized. Stir in ¾ cup dry red wine and ¾ cup malt vinegar. Continue to cook, stirring occasionally, for 30 to 35 minutes, or until mixture is thick and syrupy. Spoon into clean jars; cover and refrigerate for up to 2 weeks. Return to room temperature for serving.

DUBLINER-SPINACH-ARTICHOKE DIP

Serves 8 to 10

You'll love this dip for the slightly Mediterranean taste it gets from the marinated artichokes, the color it gets from the spinach, and the creamy texture from two cheeses — smooth cream cheese and crunchy-salty Dubliner, one of Kerrygold's most popular imports. The dip is a delicious spread on crostini, wheat crackers, or with crudité.

- 1 tablespoon olive oil
- 2 tablespoons minced shallots
- 2 (8-ounce) jars marinated artichokes, drained and chopped
- 4 tablespoon dry white wine
- 2 (10-ounce) packages frozen chopped spinach, thawed and squeezed dry
- 8 ounces cream cheese, cut into pieces
- 7 ounces Dubliner Cheese, grated
- ½ cup mayonnaise
- Dash of Tabasco sauce
- Ground black pepper
- Crostini, crackers, or crudité, for serving

1. In a large skillet over medium heat, heat olive oil. Add shallots; cook, stirring frequently, for 3 to 5 minutes, or until soft but not browned.
2. Add artichokes; cook, stirring frequently, for 5 to 7 minutes, or until warm. Add wine; cook for 3 minutes, or until evaporated. Add spinach; cook, stirring frequently, for about 3 minutes, or until blended.
3. Stir in cream cheese and Dubliner cheese; cook for 2 to 3 minutes, or until mixture is creamy. Stir in mayonnaise; season with Tabasco and pepper.
4. Transfer to a heatproof bowl. Serve at room temperature or warm in microwave for 30 to 40 seconds. Surround with vegetables, crostini, and crackers. (Dip can be made 1 day ahead; cover and refrigerate).

CORLEGGY

HARD RAW GOATS MILK CHEESE. MATURED FOR A MINIMUM 3 MONTHS. NATURAL RIND. MELLOW TASTE - STRONGER WITH AGE!

€28.00/Kg

IRISH CHEESE RAW MILK

great taste gold 2012

GOATS €10

Temple Bar Market, Dublin | *Margaret M. Johnson*

GOAT CHEESE CROSTINI WITH FIG COMPOTE

Makes 24 Crostini

CROSTINI? Bruschetta? Croûte? Whatever you call them, these little "toasts" are fantastic as a base for canapés, savory spreads, shaved meats, or cheeses. They all start with a baguette or loaf of country bread that's cut into slices, drizzled lightly with olive oil, and then baked or broiled until brown and crisp. They can be made up to two days ahead and stored in an airtight container until ready to be topped. Try these with Corleggy, goat cheese produced in Belturbet, County Cavan; St. Tola, goat cheese made at Inagh Farmhouse near Ennistymon, County Clare; or with Blue Bell Falls, goat cheese made near Charleville, County Cork. Top the crostini with this fig compote or try one of the variations that follow.

FIG COMPOTE

- ½ cup chopped dried figs
- 4 tablespoons (packed) light brown sugar
- 1 cup dry red wine
- ½ teaspoon fresh thyme
- Sea salt

CROSTINI

- 3 tablespoons extra virgin olive oil
- 1 French bread or sourdough baguette, cut into 24 (1-inch-thick) slices
- 8 ounces goat cheese

1. Make fig compote. In a small saucepan over medium heat, bring figs, sugar, wine, thyme and salt to a boil; cook for about 2 minutes. Reduce heat to simmer; cook for 8 to 10 minutes, or until mixture thickens. Cool to room temperature; cover and refrigerate for up to 2 weeks. Return to room temperature for serving.
2. Make crostini. Preheat oven to 400°F. Brush both sides of bread with olive oil. Place on a rimmed baking sheet; toast for 12 to 15 minutes, or until lightly browned.
3. To serve, spread each toast with goat cheese; top with a spoonful of compote.

GOAT CHEESE CROSTINI WITH FIG AND NUT SPREAD

Toast bread as above. In a small bowl, combine 3⁄4 cup chopped walnuts, ½ cup chopped dried figs, and 12 ounces soft goat cheese. Spread fig and nut mixture onto crostini. Sprinkle with a little chopped rosemary and drizzle lightly with balsamic glaze, preferably fig-flavored.

ROAST BEEF CROSTINI WITH GOAT CHEESE AND ROCKET

Toast bread as above. Spread soft goat cheese onto crostini. Top with two sprigs of rocket (arugula). Fold one thin slice of rare roast beef on top; season with salt and pepper. Spoon Herb Mayonnaise (page 35) on top.

GOAT CHEESE MOUSSE WITH ROASTED BEETS ON CROSTINI

Toast bread as above. In a medium bowl, whip ½ cup heavy (whipping) cream to soft peaks. In a separate bowl, whisk together 2 tablespoons milk and 4 ounces goat cheese; fold into whipped cream. Cover and refrigerate for up to 4 hours. Spread mousse onto crostini; top with a thin slice of roasted red or golden beet (page 49). Garnish with a sprig of tarragon and a few grinds of black pepper.

Elena Veselova

MINI WELLINGTONS

Makes 24

BOTH easy and elegant, these mini beef Wellingtons are perfect holiday appetizers. Use top quality beef tenderloin for best results, and for more intense flavor, mix wild and white mushrooms.

BEEF

- 2 pounds beef tenderloin, cut into 1-inch cubes
- Salt
- Ground black pepper
- 2 tablespoons extra virgin olive oil

FILLING

- 1 tablespoon extra virgin olive oil
- 1 tablespoon finely chopped shallots
- 10 ounces finely chopped white mushrooms
- Ground black pepper
- 1 tablespoon chopped fresh flatleaf parsley
- 1 teaspoon fresh thyme
- 2 sheets frozen puff pastry
- Dijon mustard, for spreading
- 1 egg beaten with 1 tablespoon water, for egg wash

1. Make beef. Toss beef with salt and pepper. In a large skillet over high heat, heat oil. Working in batches, cook beef on all sides for 1 to 2 minutes, or until seared (do not overcook). Transfer beef to paper towel-lined plate to drain; cool to room temperature.
2. Make filling. Return skillet to medium heat; heat oil. Add shallots; cook 2 to 3 minutes, or until soft but not browned. Add mushrooms; cook for 3 to 4 minutes, or until lightly browned. Stir in pepper, parsley, and thyme; cool to room temperature.
3. Preheat oven to 400°F. Line 2 baking pans with parchment paper.
4. Unfold pastry sheets; cut along fold lines into 3 strips. Cut each strip into four 3-inch squares; spread each square with mustard. Top with mushroom mixture; place a beef cube in center. Pull opposite corners of pastry into center; repeat to create a pouch. Pinch to seal. Transfer to prepared baking pans; brush with egg wash.
5. Bake for 12 to 15 minutes, or until pastry is puffed and golden. Serve warm with Herb Mayonnaise (page 35).

SMOKED SALMON PÂTÉ

Serves 6

SMOKED Irish salmon acquires its inimitable dark orange color and subtle flavor from the traditional method of smoking over an open wood fire or in a kiln. Its flavor and texture is determined by the quality of the fish, with some of the best in the world originating in pristine Irish waters. Salmon purists like nothing better than to eat it on a potato cake or on a slice of brown soda bread, but serving it as a pâté makes for great party fare.

- 4 ounces cream cheese, at room temperature
- 4 ounces crème fraîche
- 8 ounces smoked salmon
- 1 tablespoon grated lemon zest
- 1 tablespoon fresh lemon juice
- 1 tablespoon horseradish
- 2 tablespoons chopped fresh dill
- ½ teaspoon white pepper
- Brown soda bread or water crackers, for serving
- Caper berries, for garnish

1. Combine cream cheese, crème fraîche, salmon, lemon zest and juice, horseradish, dill, and pepper in a food processor; pulse 5 to 6 times, or until mixture is roughly chopped but not completely smooth.
2. Taste; adjust seasoning, adding more pepper or lemon as needed. Transfer to a Kilner jar or serving dish. (Can be made 1 day ahead; cover and refrigerate).
3. Serve with soda bread or crackers; garnish with caper berries.

Elena Veselova

TRUFFLED WILD MUSHROOM TARTLETS

Makes 15

THESE fashionable little tarts use a mix of specialty mushrooms—varieties like oyster, porcini, Portobello and enoki—and the hint of truffle oil for a distinctive earthy flavor. Tarts are easily adaptable to other fillings as well, such as leeks and blue cheese or caramelized onions and thyme (see Variations that follow). For additional servings, double, or triple the ingredients.

- 1 tablespoon canola oil
- 3 ounces mixed mushrooms, roughly chopped
- 1 tablespoon minced shallot
- 1 tablespoon white truffle oil
- 1 tablespoon minced fresh flat-leaf parsley
- 1 large egg
- ¼ cup half and half
- 2 tablespoons grated Dubliner cheese
- Ground black pepper
- 15 mini phyllo shells, or other prepared pastry cups
- Fresh chervil sprigs, for garnish

1. Preheat oven to 350°F. In a large skillet over medium heat, heat oil. Add mushrooms and shallot and cook for 3 to 4 minutes, or until mushrooms are soft but not browned. Stir in truffle oil and parsley; remove from the heat.
2. In a small bowl, whisk together egg, half and half, cheese and pepper; stir into mushroom mixture. Arrange shells on a baking sheet; divide mushroom mixture into each shell.
3. Bake for 12 to 15 minutes, or until filling is set. Remove from the oven; garnish with a sprig of chervil. Serve warm or at room temperature.

LEEK AND BLUE CHEESE TARTLETS

In a medium skillet over medium heat, heat 1 tablespoon canola oil. Add ¾ cup chopped leeks; cook for 3 to 5 minutes, or until soft but not browned. Add 2 tablespoons vegetable stock; reduce heat to simmer. Cook for about 5 minutes longer, or until most of the liquid has evaporated. Remove from heat; drain any remaining liquid. Transfer leeks to a bowl; stir in 1 large egg beaten with ½ cup half and half and ½ cup crumbled blue cheese. Season with black pepper. Divide mixture into each shell; bake as above.

CARAMELIZED ONION AND THYME TARTLETS

In a large skillet over medium heat, melt 2 ounces butter with 2 tablespoons olive oil. Stir in 3 finely chopped medium yellow onions, 1 tablespoon minced garlic, 1 tablespoon sugar, and 2 tablespoons fresh thyme leaves. Cook gently for about 20 minutes, or until onions are golden; season with sea salt and ground pepper. Cut half of a 7-ounce package Dubliner cheese into fifteen ½-inch cubes. Divide onion mixture into each shell, top with a cheese cube; bake as above. Sprinkle with additional thyme, if desired.

Bhofack2

CRAB CAKES WITH HERB MAYONNAISE

Makes 24

CRAB cakes are a great addition to a holiday party, and this flavorful mayonnaise is perfect for topping or dipping. For best results, make the sauce a few hours before serving; for a festive presentation, put the sauce in a squeeze bottle and pipe or drizzle a little on the top of each cake.

CRAB CAKES

- 8 ounces fresh crabmeat, flaked
- 1 large egg, beaten
- 2 tablespoons mayonnaise
- 1 tablespoon chopped fresh chives
- 1 tablespoon chopped fresh flatleaf parsley
- 1 teaspoon fresh tarragon
- ¼ teaspoon cayenne pepper
- 1 tablespoon fresh lemon juice
- ¼ teaspoon Worcestershire sauce
- ¼ teaspoon Tabasco sauce
- Salt
- Ground black pepper
- Seasoned breadcrumbs, for dredging
- Canola oil, for frying

HERB MAYONNAISE

- 1 cup mayonnaise
- 3 tablespoons chopped fresh chives
- 1 tablespoon chopped fresh flatleaf parsley
- 1 teaspoon chopped fresh tarragon
- 2 tablespoons fresh lemon juice
- Dash of Tabasco sauce
- Salt
- Ground black pepper

1. Make herb mayonnaise. In a medium bowl, whisk together mayonnaise, chives, parsley, tarragon, lemon juice, Tabasco, salt and pepper. (Can be made 1 day ahead; cover and refrigerate).
2. Make crab cakes. In a large bowl, combine crabmeat, egg, mayonnaise, chives, parsley, tarragon, cayenne, lemon juice, Worcestershire, Tabasco, salt and pepper; stir until blended. Shape into 24 evenly sized cakes or balls; dredge in breadcrumbs. Place on a baking sheet; cover with plastic wrap and refrigerate for 2 hours.
3. In a large skillet over medium heat, heat oil. Cook crab cakes for 3 to 5 minutes on all sides, or until golden. Remove cakes or balls from oil; drain on paper towel-lined plate.
4. Arrange cakes on serving plate; serve with mayonnaise.

Galway Farmers' Market | *Margaret M. Johnson*

MAIRGEAD MÓR/ BIG FAIR DAY

Over most of Western Europe, particularly in those areas connected with the ancient Celts, December 8 was associated with the celebration of the festival of the winter solstice. In Ireland, December 8 is also celebrated as Mairgead Mór, or the "Big Fair Day."

Brian Nolan, a Loughrea, County Galway native, remembers it as a day of great celebration, when farmers would converge on town to sell their crops, livestock, and poultry, and women would come with them to spend their "butter and egg money" on holiday gifts and goodies.

According to Nolan, "Mairgead Mór was an amazing sight to me as a child in the early 1960s, before marts and supermarkets modernized everything. On that day, everyone came to town—the ruddy-faced, wool-capped men with their sturdy womenfolk; the too-thin gaggles of wide-eyed children—on horses, in donkey and cart, on bicycles, and on foot, and everyone carried something for the fair. They arrived before dawn, and left, mess of straw and leavings behind them, after dark.

"Geese by the hundred, turkeys, and chickens by the thousand, all 'live,' tied to the back of upturned donkey carts between loads of turf. Mounds of potato sacks brimmed with Kerr's Pinks and Banners from Clare; huge heads of cabbage and turnips; bunches of parsnip and carrots, and the very rare bushel of Brussels sprouts. Wheels of hardy cheddar, and what seemed like acres of flats of eggs in hues of brown and white, with the bigger duck-eggs, bluish in the winter sunlight.

"The fowl would be raucous, hog-tied or closeted in bushel baskets, with their heads poking out, or in more modern times, poking their heads out of car-boots, and all cackling and clucking and gobbling away to their hearts' content. The 'townies' and some city market buyers made their canny way, back and forth between the rows of sellers, examining here, feeling there, commenting on the size and weight, and what they were fed on, and whether they were spring or summer birds.

"Amid all that was the excitement of the shops, the bustle of the women going in to settle their account with the harvest, butter, and turkey money enabling them to pay off the tab and get some new clothes for themselves and the children, now wide-eyed in expectation and appreciation of the beautiful goods and sweet chocolates they were able to see and touch now."

December 8 was one of the most important dates in the Celtic calendar as it marked the celebration of a farmer's success and the approach of the New Year. In modern Ireland, it's the biggest shopping day of the year.

CHAPTER TWO

BEST BEGINNINGS

STARTERS, SOUPS AND SALADS

Christmas is a time that holds all time together.
ALEXANDER SMITH, SCOTTISH POET

CHICKEN LIVER PÂTÉ WITH CRANBERRY-CUMBERLAND SAUCE

Serves 8 to 10

YOU'LL find rich pâté—whether it's made with smoked fish, chicken, duck or game livers—offered year-round in Irish restaurants, but they're more often reserved for special occasions like Christmas when they're made at home. The usual accompaniment is warm buttered toast and a piquant relish like this Cranberry-Cumberland Sauce or Red Onion Marmalade (page 23).

CHICKEN LIVER PÂTÉ

- 4 ounces butter, divided
- 3 shallots, finely chopped
- 1 tablespoon fresh thyme
- 1 pound chicken livers, rinsed and roughly chopped
- Salt
- Ground black pepper
- ¼ teaspoon ground coriander
- ¼ cup brandy or port
- ½ teaspoon ground nutmeg
- 1 tablespoon Grand Marnier
- Buttered toast or French bread, for serving
- Fresh thyme sprigs, for garnish

CRANBERRY-CUMBERLAND SAUCE

- 2 oranges
- 1 lemon
- ¼ cup port
- 1 (10-ounce) jar redcurrant jelly
- 1 cup fresh or frozen cranberries
- ½ teaspoon ground ginger
- 1 teaspoon dry mustard

1. Make pâté. In a large skillet over medium heat, heat 1 ounce of butter. Add shallots and thyme; cook for 3 minutes, or until shallots are soft but not browned. Add livers, salt, pepper, and coriander; cook for 5 minutes, stirring to cook evenly. Add brandy or port; let cook for 5 to 7 minutes, or until reduced by half. Transfer to a bowl; stir in nutmeg. Let cool completely.
2. Transfer to a food processor. Add remaining 3 ounces of butter, cut into pieces, and Grand Marnier; pulse until smooth. Adjust seasoning. Transfer to Kilner jar or bowl; cover and refrigerate for 4 hours or overnight.
3. Make cranberry-cumberland sauce. With a vegetable peeler, peel strips of zest from orange and lemon. With a sharp knife, shred zest as thinly as possible. Put zest into a small saucepan; cover with cold water. Bring to a boil. Reduce heat to simmer; cook for 5 minutes, or until zest starts to soften. Drain; reserve zest.
4. Squeeze juice from oranges and lemon into a small saucepan. Add jelly, ginger, and mustard; bring to a boil. Cook for 5 minutes; reduce heat to simmer and cook for 10 minutes, or until mixture is reduced by half. Stir in reserved zest.
5. Spoon into clean jars, cover, and refrigerate for at least 24 hours and up to 2 weeks.

Anna Shepulova

PRAWN COCKTAIL WITH MARIE ROSE SAUCE

Serves 8

Prawn cocktail, or what Americans would call shrimp cocktail, is served in Ireland and England with a mayonnaise-based sauce called Marie Rose. A bit like Russian dressing or remoulade sauce, but without the pickle relish, some recipes for the sauce call for a "touch" of ketchup and other similar ingredients like Worcestershire sauce and lemon juice; others suggest more tomato flavor from tomato purée and a bit of spice from cayenne pepper or Tabasco sauce. Adding a few slices of avocado updates this retro dish which is practically an institution during the festive season.

MARIE ROSE SAUCE

- 4 tablespoons mayonnaise
- 2 tablespoons ketchup
- 1 tablespoon extra virgin olive oil
- ½ teaspoon Dijon mustard
- 1 teaspoon horseradish
- 1 teaspoon lemon juice
- ¼ teaspoon Tabasco sauce
- ¼ teaspoon Worcestershire sauce
- Ground black pepper

COCKTAIL

- Bibb or butter lettuce
- 2 avocados, sliced
- 2 pounds large, cooked shrimp (about 48), peeled and deveined
- Lemon wedges, for serving

1. Make Marie Rose sauce. In a small bowl, whisk together mayonnaise, ketchup, olive oil, mustard, horseradish, lemon juice, Tabasco, Worcestershire and pepper; cover and refrigerate.
2. Make cocktail. Cut or shred lettuce into bite-size pieces; divide evenly into eight martini glasses or other cocktail glasses. Arrange avocado slices on top of lettuce; top with shrimp. Spoon sauce into middle of glass; garnish with lemon wedges.

Kasha Malasha

MUSHROOM AND CHESTNUT SOUP

Serves 4

THIS elegant soup is a great start to a festive feast. With earthy flavors from mushrooms and slightly sweet flavors from chestnuts, the soup is Christmas perfection.

- 2 ounces dried mushrooms
- Warm water, for soaking
- 2 tablespoons extra virgin olive oil
- 2 ounces lean bacon, chopped
- 2 shallots, finely chopped
- 1 garlic clove, finely chopped
- 3 ounces fresh white mushrooms, chopped
- 3 ounces fresh Portabello mushroom, chopped
- 2 ounces canned or vacuum-packed chestnuts, chopped
- ¼ cup dry white wine
- 4 cups homemade chicken stock or canned low-salt chicken broth
- Ground black pepper
- ½ teaspoon dried thyme
- 1 tablespoon chopped fresh flat-leaf parsley
- 1 cup heavy (whipping) cream

1. In a medium bowl, soak dried mushrooms in water for 10 minutes. Strain liquid through a paper towel-lined sieve to remove any sand or soil; cut mushrooms into pieces.
2. In a large saucepan over medium heat, heat oil. Add bacon; cook for 3 minutes. Add shallot, garlic, fresh mushrooms, chestnuts and soaked mushrooms; cook for 5 to 7 minutes, or until soft but not browned.
3. Add wine; simmer for 5 to 6 minutes, or until liquid is reduced by half. Add stock or broth, pepper, thyme and parsley. Return to simmer; continue to cook for 25 minutes, or until mushroom and chestnuts are tender.
4. Working in batches, transfer soup to a food processor or blender and process until smooth (or purée in pot with an immersion blender). Return soup to saucepan, stir in cream; simmer until heated through.
5. To serve, ladle soup into bowls.

Parsnip and Apple Soup with Parsnip Crisps

Serves 8

PARSNIPS have a unique growing season. Where other vegetables thrive in the spring and summer, the peak seasons for this hardy root vegetable are the fall and winter. Parsnips can withstand cold, even freezing temperatures, and most agree they taste better and sweeter when they're harvested after the first frost which converts starch to sugar and gives them a pleasant sweetness. When paired with a tart Granny Smith apple and aromatic spices like curry, cumin, and coriander, this soup provides an elegant start for a Christmas lunch or dinner. Top with parsnip crisps or a simple sprinkling of chives.

SOUP

- 3 ounces unsalted butter
- 1 medium onion, chopped
- 2 pounds parsnips, peeled and sliced
- 1 large Granny Smith apple, peeled, cored, and sliced
- 2 potatoes, peeled and cubed
- 6 cups homemade chicken stock or canned low-salt chicken broth
- 1 teaspoon curry powder
- 1 teaspoon ground cumin
- 1 teaspoon ground coriander
- Salt
- Ground black pepper
- ½ cup half and half
- Chopped chives, for garnish
- Parsnip Crisps, for serving

PARSNIP CRISPS

- 1 large parsnip
- 2 tablespoons canola oil, for frying
- Salt
- Ground black pepper

1. Make soup. In a large saucepan over medium heat, melt butter. Add onion and cook for 3 to 5 minutes, or until soft but not browned. Add parsnips, apples, and potato; stir to coat. Cover pan, reduce heat, and cook, stirring once or twice, for 10 to 12 minutes, or until vegetables are slightly tender.
2. Add stock or broth, curry, cumin, coriander, salt and pepper. Bring to boil; reduce heat, cover, and cook, stirring constantly, for 35 to 40 minutes, or until vegetables are tender. Let cool for 10 to 15 minutes.
3. Working in batches, transfer soup to a food processor or blender; purée until smooth (or purée in pot with an immersion blender). Return soup to saucepan, stir in half and half; simmer until heated through.
4. Make parsnip crisps. With a vegetable peeler, peel parsnip; discard peel. Continue peeling into long, thin strips. Spread strips out on a paper towel to dry slightly.
5. In a large skillet over medium heat, heat oil. Working in batches, fry strips for 2 to 3 minutes, or until strips twist up and crisp. With a slotted spoon, transfer to paper towels to drain; sprinkle with salt and pepper.
6. To serve, ladle soup into shallow bowls. Sprinkle with chives; top with crisps.

Holiday Greens with Cashel Blue, Roasted Beets, and Candied Pecans

Serves 6 to 8

The recipe for this salad comes from Kerrygold, the company that imports Irish butter and cheese to American consumers, including Cashel Blue, Ireland's first farmhouse blue cheese. It's a delicious example of the fact that not all salads are created equal! Colorful red and golden beets, blue cheese and shiny red pomegranate arils take this salad to the next level. While there's a little effort involved in roasting the beets and making the pecans (both can be done well in advance of assembling), the results are well worth it and sure to impress on the holiday table.

Candied Pecans

- 3 tablespoons light corn or golden syrup, such as Karo or Lyle's
- 1½ tablespoons sugar
- ¾ teaspoon salt
- ½ teaspoon ground black pepper
- ⅛ teaspoon cayenne pepper
- 1½ cups pecan halves

Balsamic Vinaigrette

- ¾ cup extra virgin olive oil
- ¼ cup balsamic vinegar
- 1½ tablespoons honey
- 1 teaspoon Dijon mustard
- Salt
- Ground black pepper

Salad

- 3 small golden beets
- 3 small red beets
- 2 tablespoons extra virgin olive oil
- 5 ounces mixed baby greens
- ½ cup pomegranate arils
- ½ cup candied pecans
- ½ cup crumbled Cashel Blue cheese
- ½ cup pomegranate arils

1. Make candied pecans. Preheat oven to 325°F. Coat a baking sheet with nonstick cooking spray.
2. In a large bowl, whisk together corn syrup, sugar, salt, pepper and cayenne pepper. Add pecans; stir well to coat nuts. Spread out on prepared pan.
3. Bake for 5 minutes; stir with a fork to distribute coating. Bake for 8 to 10 minutes more, or until pecans are lightly browned and coating is bubbling. Spread nuts out on another baking sheet or piece of parchment paper; quickly separate nuts before letting cool completely. (Can be stored in an airtight tin for up to 2 weeks).
4. Make balsamic vinaigrette. In a lidded jar, combine olive oil, vinegar, honey, mustard, salt and pepper; shake to blend.

Susan Vineyard

5. Make salad. Preheat oven to 400°F. Cut green tops and root ends off beets. Toss golden beets with 1 tablespoon olive oil and wrap in a foil packet. Repeat process with red beets.

6. Place beet packets on baking sheet and roast for 45 to 60 minutes, or until beets are easily pierced with the tip of a knife. (Roasting time can vary depending on the size of beets; larger ones can take up to 90 minutes to roast). Set aside until cool enough to handle. Remove beets from packets. (To prevent hands from staining, wear gloves or rubs skins off under cold running water). Cut beets into quarters.

7. In a large bowl, toss mixed greens with half the vinaigrette; toss in beets.

8. To serve, arrange greens and beets on salad plates; sprinkle with pomegranate arils, pecans, and cheese. Pass remaining vinaigrette.

Robyn Mackenzie

WINTER SALAD WITH CELERY, APPLES, AND WALNUTS

Serves 6 to 8

THIS "winter" salad is a variation of Waldorf Salad, an American dish created at New York's Waldorf Hotel (now the Waldorf-Astoria) sometime in the mid-1890s. The original recipe used apples and celery with a mayonnaise dressing, but many contemporary recipes substitute a lighter vinaigrette for the mayonnaise, like this one made with sherry vinegar and walnut oil.

SHERRY VINAIGRETTE

- 1 tablespoon minced shallots
- 2 tablespoons sherry vinegar
- Salt
- Ground black pepper
- 1 tablespoon honey
- 2 tablespoons olive oil
- 2 tablespoons walnut oil

SALAD

- 4 celery stalks, thinly sliced diagonally
- 2 Granny Smith apples, cored and thinly sliced
- 5 ounces frisée
- 1 cup roughly chopped walnuts

1. Make sherry vinaigrette. In a lidded jar, combine shallots, vinegar, salt, pepper, honey, olive oil and walnut oil; shake to blend.
2. Make salad. In a large bowl, combine celery, apples and frisée; toss with half the vinaigrette.
3. To serve, divide salad among salad plates; top with walnuts. Pass remaining vinaigrette.

Martin Turzak

CITRUS SALAD WITH BLUE CHEESE AND PECANS

Serves 8

THE mix of crunchy nuts, salty cheese and popular seedless holiday citrus like mandarins, clementines, tangerines and satsumas make this light, refreshing salad perfect for Christmas lunch. Why so popular at Christmas? Typically, these citrus varieties don't become ripe until late autumn and winter, so they're seen as a signal that Christmas is upon us. And if you've ever wondered how they became so popular as a stocking stuffer, according to legend, the fruit stands as a symbol of the gold that St. Nicholas dropped in stockings hanging by the fire.

CHAMPAGNE VINAIGRETTE

- 2 tablespoons minced shallots
- 3 tablespoons Champagne or white wine vinegar
- 1 tablespoon Dijon mustard
- 3 tablespoons extra virgin olive oil
- 2 tablespoons walnut oil
- Salt
- Ground black pepper

SALAD

- 1¼ cups pecan halves
- 5 ounces romaine, Bibb or butter lettuce, roughly torn
- 5 ounces rocket (arugula)
- Segments from 2 seedless oranges, tangerines, clementines or satsumas
- 4 ounces blue cheese, crumbled

1. Make Champagne vinaigrette. In a lidded jar, combine shallots, Champagne or white wine vinegar, mustard, olive oil, walnut oil, salt and pepper; shake well.
2. Make salad. Preheat oven to 350°F. Spread pecans out in a shallow pan; toast for about 8 minutes, or until lightly browned and fragrant. Let cool.
3. In a large bowl, combine romaine, butter lettuces, and rocket. Toss with half the vinaigrette.
4. To serve, divide salad among salad plates. Arrange citrus segments, blue cheese, and pecans on top. Pass remaining vinaigrette.

Johnnie Fox's Pub, Glencullen, Co. Dublin | *Margaret M. Johnson*

HOLIDAY TRADITIONS

A CANDLE IN THE WINDOW

During pagan festivals, candles were placed on wreaths and lit as a sign of hope that lighter days would be coming soon. Rituals were performed to help ensure the circle of life would continue, and today four candles still appear on Advent wreaths with one lit every Sunday during the month leading up to Christmas. Christmas candles and lights also owe their existence to both pagan Celtic and Christian Ireland, with ancient Celts burning them for divination and Christians burning them for religious devotion. Their use was reinforced during the years of religious persecution in Ireland when candles were put into windows to attract fugitive priests. As Alice Taylor reported in her book *The Night Before Christmas*: "The lighting of the Christmas candle marked the transition from day into night on Christmas Eve. It was the light of Christmas and the key that opened the door into the holy night." A tall, thick candle is placed on the sill of the most prominent window in the home. On Christmas Eve, the youngest child usually lights the candle, which stands as a welcoming light for neighbors, holiday visitors, and travelers like Mary and Joseph who searched for shelter and warmth. The candle also indicated a safe place for priests to perform Mass during penal times in Ireland when it was forbidden.

HANGING CHRISTMAS STOCKINGS

The tradition of hanging up stockings is linked to the Norse god Odin. While celebrating the New Year, children left food in their boots by the chimney for Odin's winged horse; Odin then swapped the food for gifts. With the arrival of Christianity, St. Nicholas and his flying reindeers took the place of Odin, and stockings replaced the boots. In Ireland, hanging Christmas stockings is a tradition in many families, but in others, children leave a pillowcase at the end of their bed to be filled with gifts.

GIVING CHRISTMAS PRESENTS

Exchanging gifts has its roots in the pagan and Roman festivals that took place at the end of the year during winter solstice. In the fourth century, St. Nicholas gained a reputation as a great gift giver, especially to children and the poor; he later became the model for Father Christmas.

FX Buckleys, Dublin | *Margaret M. Johnson*

CHAPTER THREE

THE CHRISTMAS FEAST

ROASTS, SIDES, AND SAUCES

"'Merry Christmas to you, Miss Spence. That's Nollaig shona dhuit in the old tongue.'
Kinky sniffed, then unloaded tureens and small bowls . . . Mashed potatoes, Brussels sprouts.
Carrot-and-parsnip mix. Bread sauce. Gravy.
She set a pile of dinner plates on O'Reilly's placemat. 'I'll be back with the bird.'"
PATRICK TAYLOR, *AN IRISH COUNTRY CHRISTMAS*

ROAST TURKEY

Serves 12 to 14

CHRISTMAS is the most important meal of the year in most Irish homes, and it wouldn't be the same without a turkey. But the big bird wasn't always the first choice for an Irish Christmas meal, which is generally served as a midday lunch. Until the twentieth century, goose was the number one festive food for Christmas because turkey was much more expensive than goose and generally reserved for the upper classes. In the 1950s, however, factory farming methods and freezing techniques brought turkey eating to the tables of more ordinary folk, turning the bird into a Christmas "must." The bronze turkey, a slow-rearing, free-range bird, is the premier turkey breed in Ireland. For smaller Christmas gatherings, or when a ham joins the feast (page 69), some families cook a turkey crown (breast) or turkey roulade (page 67). A few turkey tips: remember that turkeys and ovens are not created equal, so a meat thermometer should be used to ensure that both the turkey and the stuffing inside the bird reaches 165°F. Cooking times will also vary depending on whether the turkey is stuffed or unstuffed and at what temperature you use for roasting. Lastly, for best results, have the turkey and the stuffing at room temperature when you start roasting.

TURKEY

- 12- to 14-pound turkey, thawed if frozen
- 4 small onions (optional)
- 10 to 12 sprigs fresh thyme (optional)
- 2 to 3 sprigs fresh rosemary (optional)
- 1 ounce butter, at room temperature
- Salt
- Ground black pepper

GRAVY

- Reserved liquid, from drippings
- ½ cup white wine
- 4 tablespoons fat, from drippings
- 6 tablespoons flour
- Reserved stock
- Chicken broth
- Thyme sprigs (optional)
- Rosemary sprigs (optional)
- Salt
- Ground black pepper

STOCK

- Giblets, rinsed
- 1 onion, halved
- 1 carrot, cut into 2-inch pieces
- 2 to 3 sprigs fresh flatleaf parsley
- 1 celery stalk with leaves, cut into 2-inch pieces
- 1 bay leaf
- 1 tablespoon whole peppercorns

1. Make turkey. Preheat oven to 325°F. Remove package of giblets (gizzard, heart, liver, and neck) from turkey cavity; place in a saucepan for stock. Rinse neck and body cavity with cold water; pat dry. If stuffing the turkey, pack loosely into neck cavity; fasten neck skin with skewers. Fold wings across back of turkey with tips touching (to prevent burning). Loosely fill body cavity; tuck legs under band of skin at tail.

2. If not stuffing, fasten neck skin to back of turkey with a skewer; fold wings across back of turkey so tips are touching. Season cavity with salt and pepper; place onions, thyme, and rosemary in cavity.

3. Put turkey, breast-side up, on a rack in a large, shallow roasting pan. Brush skin with melted butter; season with salt and pepper.

4. Roast turkey, basting occasionally with pan drippings, for 2½ to 3 hours (if browning too quickly, cover with aluminum foil), or until a meat thermometer inserted into the thigh registers 165°F and juices run clear (internal temperature of stuffing should also register 165°F).

5. Make stock. While turkey is cooking, cover giblets with cold water; bring to a boil. Reduce heat to simmer; skim to remove surface foam. Add onion, carrot, parsley, celery, bay leaf, and peppercorns; cook, loosely covered, for 1 hour. Strain stock; let cool.

6. Remove turkey from oven. Transfer to carving board; let rest for at least 30 minutes and up to 1 hour before carving.

7. Make gravy. Pour pan drippings into a measuring cup or gravy separator. Return roasting pan to stovetop, placing pan across two burners. Deglaze pan with wine, stirring constantly to scrape up browned bits from pan. Add reserved fat; whisk in flour. Cook over medium heat, whisking constantly, for 3 to 4 minutes, or until mixture starts to thicken.

8. In a 4-cup measuring cup, combine reserved stock and enough chicken broth to fill. Pour slowly into flour mixture; continue to whisk for 5 to 8 minutes, or until gravy thickens; add thyme and rosemary sprigs, if using. Strain through a fine mesh sieve into gravy boat or bowl. Season with salt and pepper.

Fallon & Byrne, Dublin | *Margaret M. Johnson*

Turkey Talk

Roasting a turkey is the easy part of Christmas dinner—it's the issues that crop up before you roast it that are sometimes confusing. Whether to buy a fresh or frozen turkey is a matter of personal preference, but most agree there's little difference in taste unless you prefer the free-range variety where the flavor is more pronounced. If you opt for frozen, it requires careful defrosting (at least three days in its original wrapper on a tray in the refrigerator is recommended); never thaw at room temperature where increased bacterial growth and spoilage can occur. Most turkeys range in size from 8 to 24 pounds; the suggested serving size is about 1½ pounds per person. The question of cooking stuffing inside the turkey or in a casserole dish is still debatable, but more and more cooks are choosing to serve it as a side dish because the internal temperature of the stuffing might not reach a safe level of 165°F.

Turkey Timetable

Weight	Stuffed	Unstuffed
8 to 12 pounds	3 to 3½ hours	2¾ to 3 hours
12 to 14 pounds	3½ to 4 hours	3 to 3¾ hours
14 to 18 pounds	4 to 4½ hours	3¾ to 4¼ hours
18 to 20 pounds	4½ to 4¾ hours	4¼ to 4½ hours
20 to 24 pounds	4¾ to 5¼ hours	4½ to 5 hours

THREE FAVORITE STUFFINGS

Serves 10 to 12

ACCORDING to culinary historians, recipes for stuffing appeared in the oldest-known cookbook written in Rome before the first century A.D. It's doubtful that any of those recipes resemble the ones we make today, and the term generally referred to any ingredients that were used to stuff or fill meat, poultry or vegetables. In Victorian England, the word was changed to "dressing," especially for holiday meats and poultry. Nowadays, conventional wisdom suggests that it's safer to roast your holiday bird unstuffed, since the bread mixture might not reach the acceptable temperature level to effectively destroy any bacteria inside the turkey, so "dressing" has come into vogue again. Not to worry—there's little difference in taste when you bake the mixture as a side dish, and you can make one or two different dressings to satisfy even more tastes. If you prefer a softer texture, use stale white sandwich bread; if you like it with a bit more crunch, use a baguette or country loaf. Either way, you can prep the bread and cook the vegetables a day in advance and assemble on Christmas morning.

SAGE AND ONION STUFFING

- 2 baguettes, cut into bite-size pieces
- 2 ounces butter
- 1 medium onion, chopped
- 3 celery stalks, chopped
- ½ cup dry white wine
- 3 tablespoons minced fresh flatleaf parsley
- 1 tablespoon poultry seasoning

- 1 teaspoon dried sage
- 1 teaspoon celery seed
- Salt
- Ground black pepper
- 3 large eggs, beaten
- 3 cups chicken or vegetable broth

1. Preheat oven to 400°F. Coat an ovenproof baking dish with nonstick cooking spray. Arrange bread cubes on two rimmed baking sheets. Bake for about 10 minutes, or until crisp; transfer to a large bowl.
2. In a large skillet over medium heat, melt butter. Add onion and celery; cook for 5 to 7 minutes, or until soft but not browned. Add wine; cook for 3 to 5 minutes, or until nearly evaporated.
3. Toss vegetables with bread. Stir in parsley, poultry seasoning, sage, celery seed, salt, and pepper. Stir in eggs. Stir in 1½ cups of broth until bread is nearly moistened; continue to add remaining stock until bread is moist. Transfer to prepared baking dish; cover with buttered aluminum foil.
4. Bake for 45 to 50 minutes. Uncover; bake for 15 minutes longer, or until stuffing is browned.

CHESTNUT, PARSNIP, AND HERB STUFFING:

Grate 3 large parsnips; substitute parsnips for one of the baguettes. Add 1 cup crumbled cooked chestnuts. Bake as above.

MUSHROOM AND THYME STUFFING:

Add 8 ounces chopped mushrooms to celery and onions mixture; cook for 5 to 7 minutes. Substitute 1 teaspoon dried thyme for the sage. Bake as above.

Svetlana Kolpakova

TURKEY ROULADE WITH CRANBERRY AND CHESTNUT STUFFING

Serves 6 to 8

THIS butterflied turkey breast—rolled and stuffed jellyroll-style—is a smaller version of the Christmas turkey but packs the same holiday punch: lots of white meat, rich stuffing and a beautiful presentation. For the juiciest roulade, buy a boneless breast with the skin on so that the skin is rolled into the center of the turkey to help create internal moisture and to add flavor to the stuffing. A butcher will do most of the work for you, but you might want to give the breast a final flattening with a meat tenderizer or rolling pin.

CRANBERRY AND CHESTNUT STUFFING

- 2 ounces butter
- 1 cup chopped onions
- 1 cup chopped celery
- 1 cup chopped cooked chestnuts
- ½ cup dried cranberries
- 1 tablespoon fresh rosemary
- 1 tablespoon chopped fresh sage
- 1½ cups stuffing mix or bread cubes
- 1¼ to 1½ cups chicken broth
- Salt
- Ground black pepper

ROULADE

- 6-pound turkey breast, boned
- Salt
- Ground black pepper
- 1 ounce butter, at room temperature

1. Make cranberry and chestnut stuffing. In a large skillet over medium heat, melt butter. Add onions and celery; cook for 3 to 5 minutes, or until soft but not browned. Stir in chestnuts, cranberries, rosemary and sage; cook for 5 minutes.

2. Transfer mixture to a large bowl. Stir in stuffing mix or bread cubes and 1 cup of broth; add additional broth until bread is moistened. Season with salt and pepper.

3. Make roulade. Preheat oven 325°F. Lay out butterflied breast, skin-side down, on parchment paper; sprinkle with salt and pepper. Spread stuffing in an even layer onto breast, leaving a small border on all sides. (Place excess stuffing in a buttered baking dish; cook during last 45 minutes of roasting the turkey). Roll turkey up tightly; place seam-side down on parchment. With kitchen twine, tie up breast at 2-inch intervals; tie up lengthwise. Spread all over with butter; season with salt and pepper. Lift roulade and parchment onto a baking pan.

4. Roast for 1 hour and forty-five minutes to 2 hours, or until an instant-read thermometer registers 150°F in center. Remove from oven; cover with aluminum foil. Let rest for about 15 minutes before carving into ½-inch-thick slices.

GLAZED HOLIDAY HAM

Serves 12 to 14

Ham is a classic Christmas dish, often served alongside the turkey with at least two types of potatoes and any number of side dishes from roasted parsnips to Brussels sprouts and red cabbage. Many cooks prefer to buy a fully cooked ham that requires only roasting and glazing, but a traditional Christmas ham in Ireland generally starts as gammon, a piece of pork that's cured but needs to be cooked first; when cooked it becomes ham. It's boiled first, skinned, and then roasted and glazed. A whole Irish ham can weigh up to twenty pounds, but butchers will cut one and sell in a smaller size to suit. (For where to buy an authentic Irish ham in the United States, see NOTE).

HAM

- 10-pound fresh ham
- 1 large carrot, chopped
- 1 celery stalk, chopped
- 1 onion, halved
- 1 bay leaf
- 1 tablespoon peppercorns
- 1 orange, thickly sliced
- 4 cups cider
- 4 cups water
- Whole cloves, for studding

GLAZE

- 3 tablespoons light brown sugar
- 3 tablespoons honey
- ½ teaspoon ground nutmeg
- 1 teaspoon Dijon mustard
- ⅔ cup orange juice

1. Make ham. Put ham, carrot, celery, onion, bay leaf, peppercorns, and orange into a large pot; cover with cider and water. Bring to a boil; reduce heat, cover, and simmer for about 2 hours (cook 22 to 25 minutes per pound), or until tender. Skim foam from surface 2 to 3 times during cooking. Remove pan from heat; let ham cool in cooking liquid.
2. Make glaze. In a small saucepan over medium heat, combine brown sugar, honey, nutmeg, mustard and orange juice. Cook for 5 to 10 minutes, stirring constantly, until thick and smooth.
3. Preheat oven 450° F. Remove ham from pan; pat dry. Transfer to a roasting pan. With a sharp knife, remove skin, leaving layer of fat. Score diagonally to make a diamond pattern; stud each diamond with cloves. Brush glaze over the ham.
4. Bake for 25 to 30 minutes, until golden browned. Remove ham from oven; let rest for at least 15 minutes before slicing.

NOTE: Two online sites in the United States that sell authentic Irish foods, including ham, are www.foodireland.com and www.tommymoloneys.com.

Midleton Farmers' Market, Co. Cork | *Margaret M. Johnson*

ROASTED POTATOES

Serves 8 to 10

Roasted potatoes are a Christmas "must." For perfect roast potatoes with a crisp golden crust, the most important things to remember are to use a floury variety—in Ireland, the most popular ones bear names like Kerrs Pinks, Maris Pipers, and Roosters, to name a few—and to not roast them too far in advance as they lose their crunch if you keep them waiting. Outside of Ireland, the best substitute for a floury Irish variety is a Russet or Idaho, both of which have a high starch content and floury texture. For best results, resist the temptation to make ahead; once potatoes are crisp, serve them as soon as possible.

- 4 pounds floury potatoes, peeled and cut into egg-size pieces or quarters
- 3 tablespoons olive oil or duck fat
- Sea salt
- Ground black pepper

1. In a large saucepan, cover potatoes with cold salted water; bring to a boil. Cook for 10 to 12 minutes, or until nearly tender (do not overcook); drain. When cool enough to handle, scratch surface of each potato with a fork; shake them in the pan (this will contribute to a crispy texture).
2. Preheat oven to 350°F. Heat oil or fat in a roasting pan until sizzling. Add potatoes; toss to evenly coat. Sprinkle with salt and pepper. Cook in a single layer, turning once or twice, for 30 to 40 minutes, or until brown and crisp.
3. Remove from oven; drain fat. Keep in warm oven, uncovered; season again with salt and pepper.

BUTTERY MASHED POTATOES

Serves 8 to 10

- 4 pounds floury potatoes, peeled and cut into 1½-inch pieces
- ¾ cup heavy (whipping) cream
- ¾ cup milk
- 2 ounces butter
- 2 tablespoons minced fresh sage
- Salt
- Ground black pepper

1. In a large saucepan, cover potatoes with cold salted water; bring to a boil. Cook for 18 to 20 minutes, or until tender; drain. Press potatoes through a ricer; return to saucepan.
2. In a small saucepan over medium heat, heat cream and milk. Stir in butter and sage; cook for 2 to 3 minutes, or until butter melts.

3. Stir cream mixture into mashed potatoes; season with salt and pepper. Transfer to a buttered ovenproof baking dish. (Can be made 2 days ahead; cover and refrigerate. Bring to room temperature before baking).
4. Preheat oven to 350°F. Bake potatoes, covered, for about 30 minutes. Uncover, bake 10 minutes longer, or until heated through.

DAUPHINOISE POTATOES

Serves 8

A WAXY potato—one with a medium starch content and creamy texture, such as Yukon Gold—is great for an elegant gratin like this.

- 2¼ cups heavy (whipping) cream
- 2¼ cups milk
- 3 garlic cloves
- 8 large waxy potatoes, peeled and thinly sliced
- Salt
- Ground black pepper
- 4 ounces grated Swiss cheese

1. Preheat oven to 375°F. Coat an ovenproof gratin dish with butter flavor cooking spray.
2. In a large saucepan over medium heat, bring cream, milk and garlic to simmer. Stir in potatoes; cook, stirring gently to prevent sticking, for 8 to 10 minutes, or until tender when pierced with the tip of a sharp knife.
3. With a slotted spoon, transfer potatoes to the prepared dish. Pour cream over potatoes, discarding garlic. Season with salt and pepper; sprinkle with cheese.
4. Bake for 50 to 55 minutes, or until potatoes are tender and top is browned and crisp.

BRUSSELS SPROUTS WITH BACON

Serves 8 to 10

L IKE many foods, Brussels sprouts are nearly obligatory on the Christmas menu. Sprouts look like little cabbages (they're in the same family but grow differently) and can be remarkably delicious when sautéed or stir-fried with bacon or prosciutto and a touch of garlic. For best results, remove any limp outer leaves and trim the stem end. Slicing the sprouts lengthwise helps them cook more quickly.

- 20 ounces Brussels sprouts, trimmed and halved
- 2 ounces bacon or prosciutto, chopped
- 3 tablespoons extra virgin olive oil

- 1 tablespoon chopped garlic
- Salt
- Ground black pepper

1. In a large saucepan over medium heat, cook Brussels sprouts in boiling salted water for 3 minutes, or until crisp; drain.
2. In a large skillet over medium heat, cook bacon or prosciutto for 6 to 7 minutes, or until crisp; transfer to paper towel-lined plate to drain.
3. Return skillet to medium heat; heat oil. Add garlic; cook for 1 to 2 minutes, or until soft but not browned. Add Brussels sprouts; cook for 4 to 5 minutes, or until lightly browned. Remove from the heat; stir in bacon. Season with salt and pepper.

BRAISED RED CABBAGE WITH APPLES

Serves 8 to 10

FRUITY, spicy, and tart dishes like this complement the rich flavor of both turkey and ham. This one-pot dish can be assembled and cooked while the meat is roasting.

- 4 slices bacon, cut into 1-inch pieces
- 1 medium onion, thinly sliced
- 1 large red cabbage, halved, cored, and thinly sliced
- 2 tart apples, peeled, cored, and chopped
- ½ cup sultanas (golden raisins)
- Zest of 1 small orange
- 1/2 cup (packed) light brown sugar
- 1 cinnamon stick
- ¾ cup red wine
- 3 tablespoons red wine vinegar
- Salt
- Ground black pepper

1. In a large saucepan over medium heat, cook bacon for 7 to 8 minutes, or until crisp; transfer to paper towel-lined plate to drain. Add onion; cook, stirring frequently, for 3 to 5 minutes, or until soft but not browned.
2. Add cabbage to saucepan; stir to coat. Stir in apples, sultanas, orange zest, brown sugar, cinnamon stick, wine and vinegar. Bring to a boil; cover and cook for 5 minutes.
3. Reduce heat; simmer, covered, for 50 to 60 minutes, or until cabbage is very tender. Season with salt and pepper. (Can be made 1 day ahead; cover and refrigerate).

ROASTED WINTER VEGETABLES

Serves 8 to 10

A MEDLEY of roasted winter vegetables is a tasty accompaniment to a holiday roast. Once the hard work of peeling and cutting is finished (most of the vegetables can be prepared beforehand and stored in resealable bags in the refrigerator), it literally becomes a one-pot dish. Roasting times vary a bit, so add the vegetables at the suggested intervals.

- 4 large carrots, cut into 2-inch pieces
- 1 large rutabaga (yellow turnip or Swede), cut into 1-inch pieces
- 2 large parsnips, cut into 2-inch pieces
- 1 pound baby or fingerling potatoes, halved
- 1 large celeriac (celery root), cut into 1-inch pieces
- 1 large onion, quartered
- 4 garlic cloves, chopped
- ⅓ cup olive oil
- Salt
- Ground black pepper
- 2 to 3 sprigs fresh rosemary
- 2 to 3 leeks (white part only), washed thoroughly, cut into 1-inch pieces
- 1 bulb sweet fennel, quartered (optional)
- 2 tablespoons white balsamic vinegar

1. Preheat oven to 350°F. Place carrots, rutabaga, parsnips, potatoes, celeriac, onion, and garlic in a large roasting pan; toss with olive oil, salt, pepper, and rosemary.
2. Roast for 15 minutes, toss once; add leeks and fennel (if using). Roast for 40 to 45 minutes longer, or until all vegetables are browned and tender when pierced with the tip of a sharp knife; remove from oven. Transfer vegetables to a serving dish; drizzle with vinegar.

CLASS 1

PARSNIPS
PER KG

CLASS 1
CARROTS
£2.90 PER KG

ROASTED PARSNIPS AND CARROTS WITH HONEY-MUSTARD GLAZE

Serves 8 to 10

- 2 pounds parsnips, peeled, halved lengthwise
- 1 pound carrots, peeled, halved lengthwise
- 4 tablespoons olive oil
- Salt
- Ground black pepper
- 2 tablespoons wholegrain mustard
- 3 tablespoons honey

1. In a large saucepan over medium heat, cook parsnips and carrots in boiling salted water for 5 minutes, or until nearly tender when pierced with the tip of a sharp knife; drain.
2. Preheat oven to 400°F. Place vegetables in a large roasting pan; toss with olive oil, salt and pepper. Roast for 30 minutes, tossing once or twice, or until lightly browned and tender. Transfer to an ovenproof baking dish.
3. In a small bowl, whisk together mustard and honey; brush over vegetables. Return to oven; roast for 10 minutes longer, or until browned and glazed.

PARSNIP AND TURNIP PURÉE

Serves 8 to 10

- 3 pounds parsnips, peeled and cut into 1-inch pieces
- 1 pound turnip, peeled and cut into 1-inch pieces
- 4 ounces butter, at room temperature
- ½ teaspoon nutmeg
- ½ cup minced flatleaf parsley
- Salt
- Ground black pepper

1. In a large saucepan, cover parsnips and turnip with cold salted water; bring to a boil. Cook for 30 to 40 minutes, or until tender; drain and mash.
2. Transfer to a food processor. Add butter, nutmeg, and parsley; process until smooth. Transfer to a serving bowl; season with salt and pepper.

Svetlana Kolpakova

CRANBERRY-ORANGE RELISH

Makes 2 Cups

No Christmas meal is complete without the tangy taste of cranberry sauce, relish, or chutney. Simple sauce (cranberries, sugar, and water) is delicious enough; additions like dates, figs, orange juice, nuts—you name it—elevate it to sublime. A recipe for Cranberry-Cumberland Sauce also appears on page 41.

- ½ cup water
- ½ cup orange juice
- 1 cup sugar
- 12 ounces fresh or frozen cranberries
- 2 cinnamon sticks
- Pinch of salt
- 2 tablespoons grated orange zest

1. In a medium saucepan over medium heat, bring water, orange juice, and sugar to a boil. Add cranberries; return to boiling. Reduce heat; add cinnamon sticks, salt, and orange zest. Simmer, stirring occasionally, for 8 to 10 minutes, or until cranberries burst.
2. Remove from heat; let cool to room temperature. (Cover and refrigerate for up to 2 weeks). Serve at room temperature.

CRANBERRY CHUTNEYS

CRANBERRY-WALNUT CHUTNEY

In a large saucepan, bring 12 ounces fresh or frozen cranberries, ⅔ cup (packed) light brown sugar, ⅓ cup chopped dates, ⅓ cup chopped celery, ½ Granny Smith apple (cored and diced), ½ small, finely chopped onion, 1 tablespoon crystallized ginger (diced), ¼ cup water, and 1 tablespoon fresh lemon juice to a boil. Reduce heat to medium-low; cook, stirring occasionally, for 15 to 20 minutes, or until mixture thickens. Remove from heat; let cool to room temperature. (Cover and refrigerate for up to 2 weeks). Just before serving time, stir in ½ cup chopped walnuts. Serve at room temperature.

CRANBERRY-GINGER CHUTNEY

In a large saucepan, bring 12 ounces fresh or frozen cranberries, ½ cup dried cranberries, 1 Granny Smith apple (cored and diced), 1-inch piece fresh ginger (peeled and diced), 1 cup apple juice, 1 cup sugar, and 4 whole cloves to a boil. Reduce heat to medium-low; cook, stirring occasionally, for 15 minutes, or until mixture thickens. Remove from heat; let cool to room temperature. (Cover and refrigerate for up to 2 weeks). Serve at room temperature.

The Garden, Dublin | Jeri Glasgow

HOLIDAY TRADITIONS

DECORATING WITH EVERGREENS AND WREATHS

The tradition of using evergreens at Christmas has pagan and Roman roots, with a wreath of evergreen foliage used during mid-winter festivals to symbolize victory of life over darkness. The wreath represented the circle of life that starts again every spring and bringing greenery into the home was also thought to protect it from evil spirits, demons, and witches who were thought to be afraid of the color green. Because holly flourishes at this time of year, even the poor had means to decorate their homes. All decorations are traditionally taken down on January 6, also known as The Feast of the Epiphany or Little Christmas, and it's considered bad luck to take them down before that date.

DECORATING THE TREE

The custom of decorating a fir tree can be traced back to Roman times, but a popular legend suggests that in eighth-century Germany, St. Boniface cut down an oak tree worshipped by pagans and a fir tree sprung up from its roots. The pagans converted to Christianity and decorated the tree to celebrate Christmas rather than the winter solstice. Decorating a tree with fruit and candles can be seen as both pagan and Christian, with decorations originally used to symbolize the fruits of the earth (baubles or ornaments) and the fiery sun (tinsel). The tradition became popular in Europe, and Prince Albert introduced it into England in the mid-nineteenth century. During the nearly seventy years of her reign, Queen Victoria presided over a resurgence of the Christmas celebration, and an illustration of her family around their Christmas tree in December 1860 inspired her subjects to follow her example with a decorated tree of their own.

MISTLETOE

From the earliest times, mistletoe has been one of the most magical, mysterious, and sacred plants in European folklore. It was thought to bestow life and fertility and to be a protection against poison as well as an aphrodisiac. The Druids, the old Irish pre-Christian priests, revered mistletoe for its ability to survive and remain green throughout the winter despite having no roots, and they harvested it during the winter solstice for medicinal use. Hanging a bough of mistletoe at the beginning of the Christmas season became a popular tradition, and young men were permitted to kiss any girl they managed to draw under the bough. The kiss underneath was thought to lead to a year of good luck.

CHAPTER FOUR

ELEGANT ENDINGS

BEST CHRISTMAS SWEETS

Christmas is not an external event at all,
But a piece of one's home that one carries in one's heart.
FREYA STARK, ENGLISH WRITER

Kuvona

MINCEMEAT

Makes 2 cups

MINCEMEAT, a mixture of chopped dried fruits, spices, and spirits, is one of Ireland's most popular Christmas foods. It was developed more than 500 years ago in England as a way of preserving meat without salting or smoking and was esteemed as holiday fare there during the era of Henry VII, who proclaimed Christmas a day of feasting. Some early recipes for mincemeat used suet, veal, or mutton, and gradually cooks added ingredients like apples, Seville oranges, and even red wine. When there was no longer any need to preserve meat with honey or spices, the meat in mincemeat was eliminated and replaced with fruit alone, although some cooks still use a bit of suet in their recipes. In Elizabethan England, huge mince pies were made during the Twelve Days of Christmas, and it became customary to offer a visiting guest a slice. The leap from England to Ireland was a short one, and mincemeat soon became a favorite ingredient in an Irish Christmas as well, especially in the form of little mince pies. Along with steamed pudding and fruitcake, mincemeat has been the standard-bearer of traditional Christmas desserts in Ireland, the United Kingdom, and elsewhere for centuries.

- ¼ cup sultanas (golden raisins)
- ¼ cup currants
- ¼ cup raisins
- ¼ cup candied mixed peel, chopped
- 2 tablespoons chopped candied cherries
- Grated zest and juice of 1 lemon
- Grated zest and juice of 1 orange
- 1 Granny Smith apple, cored and shredded
- ¼ cup (packed) dark brown sugar
- 2 teaspoons Mixed Spice (page 92) or pumpkin pie spice
- 2 tablespoons fresh white breadcrumbs
- 3 tablespoons brandy
- 2 tablespoons dark rum

1. In a large bowl, combine sultanas, currants, raisins, minced peel, cherries, lemon zest and juice, orange zest and juice, apple, brown sugar, Mixed Spice or pumpkin pie spice, breadcrumbs, brandy, and rum; stir thoroughly. Cover; let stand at room temperature for at least 24 hours. Stir in additional brandy or rum, if desired.
2. Spoon into clean jars; cover and refrigerate for up to 2 weeks.

MINCEMEAT TARTS

Makes 12 tarts

T HESE star-studded little tarts are the stuff of which Christmas is made. They start appearing in Irish supermarkets as early as November, and they're so beloved, many families have to replenish their supply a few times before Christmas. For cooks who prefer to make their own, you can cover the tops with a small star instead of a full top crust. For an additional twist, add a topping of almond cream to make Frangipane Mince Pies and serve them with Brandy Butter (page 89).

PASTRY

- 2 cups flour
- ½ cup ground almonds
- 5 ounces chilled unsalted butter, cut into small pieces
- Grated zest of 1 orange
- ¼ cup sugar
- 1 large egg yolk
- 3 tablespoons ice water

FILLING

- 1 cup homemade or prepared mincemeat
- 1 large egg white, beaten
- Confectioners' sugar, for dusting

1. Make pastry. Combine flour, almonds, butter, zest, and sugar in a food processor. Pulse 8 to 10 times, or until mixture resembles coarse crumbs. Add egg yolk and water; process for 20 to 30 seconds, or until dough comes together.
2. Form dough into a ball and then flatten into a disk. Cover with plastic wrap; refrigerate for 30 minutes.
3. Preheat oven to 350°F. Dust a work surface with flour. Return dough to floured surface; roll out to a ⅛-inch-thick round. With a 3-inch cookie cutter, cut out 12 rounds. Put rounds into cups of 1 standard cupcake pan. Reroll scraps; with a star-shaped cookie cutter, cut out 12 small stars.
4. Spoon mincemeat into pastry shells; top each with a star. Brush stars and tart edges with egg white.
5. Bake for 28 to 30 minutes, or until pastry is golden and filling is bubbling. Transfer to a wire rack; let cool for about 10 minutes. Sprinkle with confectioners' sugar before serving.

FRANGIPANE MINCEMEAT TARTS

Prepare tarts through step 3. For the frangipane, beat 2 ounces softened butter and ¼ cup sugar with an electric mixer on medium speed until light and fluffy. Add 1 egg; beating well. Beat in ¼ cup flour and ¼ cup ground almonds until smooth. Spoon mincemeat into pastry shells; top with frangipane. Top each with a star. Brush stars and tart edges with egg white. Bake as above.

CRANBERRIES
250g £4.50

Belfast City Hall Christmas Market | *Northern Ireland Tourist Board*

CRANBERRY-MINCEMEAT PUFFS

Makes 15

MINCEMEAT and cranberries, two of the season's most beloved ingredients, combine beautifully in these little "puffs" made with prepared puff pastry (ready rolled or frozen), such as Pepperidge Farm or Dufour in the United States, or Jus-Rol in Ireland and the United Kingdom. Like the mincemeat tarts on page 87, these little sweets are topped with a festive pastry star and dusted with confectioners' sugar. Serve the puffs with Brandy Butter or make Brandy Butter Ice Cream (recipes follows).

- 1 sheet frozen puff pastry, defrosted according to package directions
- 1 cup homemade or prepared mincemeat
- 1 cup fresh or frozen cranberries
- 2 tablespoons granulated sugar
- 1 egg white, beaten, for brushing
- Confectioners' sugar, for dusting

1. Preheat oven to 400°F. Line a baking sheet with parchment paper.
2. Unroll pastry sheet. Cut a 2½-inch strip off of one end; with a small star-shaped cutter, cut out 12 stars. Cut remaining pastry into 3 rows by 5 rows to make 15 squares. Score ½ inch from each edge.
3. In a medium bowl, combine mincemeat, cranberries, and sugar. Spoon mixture into center of each square; top with a star. Brush edges with egg white.
4. Arrange squares on prepared pan; bake for 12 to 15 minutes, or until puffed and golden. Let cool on a wire rack. Dust with confectioners' sugar; serve warm or at room temperature.

BRANDY BUTTER

In a medium bowl, beat 4 ounces unsalted butter and 1½ cups confectioners' sugar with an electric mixer on medium speed until light and fluffy. Add 2 tablespoons brandy; beat until smooth. Transfer to a small bowl or jar. (Cover and refrigerate for up to 2 weeks). Return to room temperature for serving.

BRANDY BUTTER ICE CREAM

In a medium bowl, beat 1 cup brandy butter and 2 cups sweetened condensed milk with an electric mixer on medium speed until smooth. In another medium bowl, beat 3 cups heavy (whipping) cream with an electric mixer on high speed until soft peaks form. Fold into brandy butter mixture; fold in 1 tablespoon orange zest. Transfer mixture to a freezer-proof container, cover, and freeze for 24 hours. Remove from freezer 10 minutes before serving.

Tomas24

CHRISTMAS PUDDING

Serves 10 to 12

THE original "figgy pudding," created sometime in the 1400s, was a dish of dried figs, dates, raisins, and spices boiled in almond milk. Also called "plum pudding"—despite the fact that it contains no plums whatsoever—this steamed or boiled pudding was first recorded as "Christmas Pudding" in 1858 in a novel by British author Anthony Trollope. The name is probably derived from the substitution of raisins for dried plums as an ingredient in pies during medieval times. In the sixteenth and seventeenth centuries, dishes made with raisins retained the term "plum," and in the Victorian era, Christmas plum puddings became a well-loved dessert. Curiously, plum pudding was a latecomer to Ireland, but it caught on quickly and today it's one of the best loved Christmas desserts. Not to be confused with fruitcake, it's actually more like a dense spice cake. To lighten it up, make Cranberry Christmas Pudding (recipe follows) and serve the puddings with Brandy Butter (page 89), the quintessential topping for Christmas puddings.

- 1 cup sultanas (golden raisins)
- 1 cup currants
- ¼ cup chopped dried figs
- ¼ cup chopped dried apricots
- ¼ cup candied cherries, halved
- ¼ cup mixed candied peel
- ⅓ cup brandy or dark rum
- Grated zest and juice of 1 orange
- 4 ounces unsalted butter, at room temperature
- ½ cup (packed) dark brown sugar
- 3 large eggs, beaten
- ¼ cup chopped stem ginger
- 1 apple, peeled, cored, and grated
- 1¼ cups flour
- 1 cup fresh white breadcrumbs
- 1 teaspoon Mixed Spice (see NOTE) or pumpkin pie spice
- 1 teaspoon ground cinnamon

1. In a large bowl, combine sultanas, currants, figs, apricots, cherries, and mixed peel. Add brandy or rum, orange zest, and juice. Cover; let stand at room temperature overnight.
2. Coat a 6-cup pudding mold or deep, heatproof bowl with butter flavor cooking spray; place a round of wax paper on bottom. In a large bowl, beat butter and sugar with an electric mixer on medium speed until light and fluffy; gradually beat in eggs. Stir in soaked fruits, ginger, apple, flour, breadcrumbs, Mixed Spice, and cinnamon.
3. Spoon mixture into prepared mold; smooth top. Cover with a double piece of buttered wax paper and a double piece of aluminum foil. Fold together to make a pleat in center (to allow pudding to expand). Tie paper and foil in place with kitchen twine.

4. Place mold or dish into a large saucepan or Dutch oven fitted with a rack or put a folded kitchen towel on bottom of the pot (to prevent direct contact with bottom of pot). Add enough hot water to pot to come halfway up sides of mold or dish.

5. Cover and steam on medium-low heat for 2 to 2 and a half hours, or until a skewer inserted into center comes out clean. (Check water level once or twice during cooking; add more water when necessary.)

6. With oven mitts to protect your hands, carefully remove pudding from saucepan. Remove foil and parchment; run a metal spatula around sides to loosen. Place a serving plate over mold and invert pudding; let cool for about 15 minutes. Slice and serve warm with Brandy Butter.

7. If not serving immediately, let pudding cool completely. Wrap in plastic wrap and then aluminum foil. Refrigerate pudding for up to 1 week or freeze. To reheat, return pudding to mold, cover with wax paper or foil; steam for 1 hour, as above, or until heated through. (Thaw frozen pudding before reheating as above.)

NOTE: To make Mixed Spice, put 1 tablespoon coriander seeds, 1 crushed cinnamon stick, 1 teaspoon whole cloves, and 1 teaspoon allspice berries in a spice or coffee grinder; process until finely ground. Add 1 tablespoon ground nutmeg and 2 teaspoons ground ginger; stir to blend. Store in an airtight container.

CRANBERRY CHRISTMAS PUDDING

Coat a 6-cup pudding mold or deep, heatproof bowl with butter flavor cooking spray; place a round of wax paper on bottom. In a large bowl, whisk together 1½ cups flour, ½ teaspoon salt, ½ teaspoon baking powder, ¼ teaspoon baking soda, ¼ teaspoon ground nutmeg, and ¼ teaspoon ground cinnamon. In a large bowl, combine 5 tablespoons molasses (dark treacle), 4 tablespoons sugar, 2 tablespoons dark rum, and 2 tablespoons canola oil; stir well. Stir in 1 Granny Smith apple, peeled, cored and coarsely chopped, 1 cup fresh or frozen cranberries, coarsely chopped, and ¼ cup raisins. Stir in flour mixture until blended. Spoon into prepared mold; steam as above.

CHRISTMAS PUDDING ICE CREAM

Serves 8 to 10

I_F_ "Christmas comes but once a year" so, too, does Christmas pudding. To make it last a bit longer, turn any leftovers into this long lasting, crunchy ice cream that you can eat well into the new year.

- ○ 2 cups crumbled Christmas pudding, divided
- ○ 1 tablespoon brandy
- ○ 2 tablespoons light brown sugar
- ○ 2 cups heavy (whipping) cream
- ○ 2 cups milk
- ○ 1 tablespoon vanilla bean paste
- ○ 2 large egg yolks
- ○ ½ cup sugar
- ○ 2 tablespoons vanilla extract

1. Preheat oven to 300°F. Line a baking sheet with parchment paper.
2. In a small bowl, combine 1 cup crumbled pudding with brandy; toss to coat.
3. Put remaining 1 cup of crumbs on baking sheet. Sprinkle with brown sugar; toss to coat. Bake for 12 to 15 minutes, tossing once or twice, or until lightly browned and crisp. Let cool completely.
4. In a medium saucepan over medium heat, bring cream, milk, and vanilla bean paste nearly to a boil; reduce heat to simmer.
5. In a small bowl, beat egg yolks, sugar, and vanilla extract with an electric mixer on medium speed until pale and smooth. Whisk in 4 tablespoons cream mixture until blended. Gradually add egg yolk mixture back into cream mixture, whisking continuously to prevent eggs from curdling. Cook over low heat for 3 to 4 minutes, or until mixture thickens and coats back of a spoon. Remove from heat; let cool completely.
6. Pour mixture into bowl of an ice cream maker; stir in crumbled pudding mixture. Let churn for 20 to 25 minutes, or until mixture thickens. Transfer ice cream to a freezer proof container; fold in crisp pudding mixture. Cover and freeze overnight.

Peter Goskov

CHRISTMAS CAKE

Serves 10 to 12

This is the "Great Irish Cake," the pièce de résistance into which every Irish cook sinks her reputation. Spiced, sweet desserts like this cake have been a part of Irish holiday celebrations for centuries and were highly prized because they included spices and dried fruits, once difficult and expensive to obtain. The cake is generally covered with marzipan, which provides a lovely almond flavor and helps to keep the cake moist, and topped with either fondant or Royal Icing. Many cooks like to take on the added chore of making their own marzipan and fondant, but if you're like me and look to save some time during the busy season, excellent ready to roll products are available (Dr. Oetker, Renshaw and Shamrock brands in Ireland, Odense, Solo and Wilton in the U.S. are good choices). An alternative to fondant is Royal Icing (recipe follows). Decorate the cake with marzipan stars or leaves, gold or silver sugar pearl sprinkles, or Sugared Cranberries and Rosemary (recipe follows).

CAKE

- 2 cups dried currants
- 2 cups sultanas (golden raisins)
- 1 cup raisins
- ¼ cup candied cherries
- ¼ cup candied mixed peel
- ¾ cup chopped almonds
- Grated zest and juice of 1 lemon
- 1½ teaspoon Mixed Spice (page 92) or pumpkin pie spice
- ½ teaspoon ground nutmeg
- 1 cup Irish whiskey, divided
- 8 ounces butter, at room temperature
- 1 cup (packed) dark brown sugar
- 5 large eggs
- 2 cups flour, sifted

MARZIPAN

- ¼ cup apricot jam, heated
- 1 (454g) package marzipan

ROYAL ICING

- 2 large egg whites
- 3¼ cups confectioners' sugar, sifted
- 2 teaspoons fresh lemon juice

1. Make cake. The day before baking, combine currants, sultanas, raisins, cherries, mixed peel, almonds, lemon zest and juice, Mixed Spice or pumpkin pie spice, nutmeg, and ½ cup of whiskey in a large bowl. Cover; let stand at room temperature overnight.
2. Preheat oven to 275°F. Coat a 9-inch springform pan with baking spray with flour; line bottom and sides with parchment paper.
3. In the bowl of a stand mixer fitted with the paddle attachment (or with a hand mixer), beat butter and sugar on medium speed until light and fluffy. Add eggs, one at a time, beating in thoroughly and adding ¼ cup flour with each egg. Fold in remaining flour; stir in soaked fruit. Transfer mixture to prepared pan.

4. Bake for 2 hours to 2 hours and fifteens minutes, or until a skewer inserted into center comes out clean. Remove from oven; let cool in pan on a wire rack for 30 minutes.

5. Prick top of cake with a skewer in several places; spoon or brush remaining ½ cup whiskey over top. Release sides of pan. Invert cake onto rack; remove pan bottom and lining paper. Let cool completely. Wrap cake in parchment paper and tape it closed. Wrap in aluminum foil. Store in a cool place for several weeks to allow cake to mature. Unwrap cake every week; brush a few tablespoons of Irish whiskey on top. Rewrap.

6. Prepare marzipan. On day before serving, lightly dust a work surface with sugar. Unwrap cake; brush top and sides with apricot jam. Knead marzipan until it's softy and pliable. Lightly dust work surface and rolling pin with confectioners' sugar. Roll out marzipan to a round large enough to cover top and sides of cake. Lift marzipan using rolling pin; drape over cake. With your hands, start in center and smooth marzipan over top to edges and down sides, pressing out any air bubbles. With a sharp knife, trim excess. Cover cake with a clean tea towel and let dry overnight.

7. Make royal icing. In a stand mixer fitted with the whisk attachment (or with a hand medium- mixer), beat egg whites on high speed for 5 to 6 minutes, or until glossy peaks form. Add confectioners' sugar and lemon juice; beat for about 1 minute longer, or mixture is stiff enough to spread. With a flexible rubber spatula, spread icing over top and sides of cake. Decorate top with sugared cranberries and rosemary, if desired. Let icing dry and harden for at least 24 hours. If using ready-to-roll fondant, follow directions on package.

SUGARED CRANBERRIES AND ROSEMARY

In a small saucepan over medium heat, combine 1 cup water and ½ cup sugar. Cook for 4 to 5 minutes, or until sugar dissolves; remove from heat. Add ½ cup cranberries; stir to coat in syrup. With a slotted spoon, transfer cranberries to a wire rack set over a baking sheet or paper towels to drain excess syrup. Let dry for 30 to 40 minutes. Roll in additional sugar; return to rack to dry completely. Repeat with rosemary sprigs. Store in a single layer in an airtight tin; refrigerate for up to 2 weeks.

PEAR AND GINGER PUDDING

Serves 6 to 8

THIS pudding is a riff on steamed pudding and gingerbread. It starts with gooey pears on the bottom and finishes when the cake is turned upside down to reveal them as a deliciously gooey top! In between is a rich, dark, and spicy ginger cake that simply begs to be topped with whipped or clotted cream!

- 4 ounces unsalted butter, divided
- ½ cup (packed) light brown sugar
- 1 (15-ounce) can sliced pears in fruit juice, drained
- ½ cup sultanas (golden raisins)
- 1 cup all-purpose flour
- ½ teaspoon baking soda
- 1 teaspoon ground cinnamon
- ½ teaspoon ground ginger
- Pinch of ground cloves
- Pinch of ground nutmeg
- 1 large egg, beaten
- ¼ cup (packed) dark brown sugar
- ⅓ cup golden syrup, such as Lyle's, or light corn syrup
- ⅔ cup milk
- Confectioners' sugar, for dusting
- Whipped or clotted cream, for serving

1. Preheat oven to 350°F. Line an 8-inch round baking pan with parchment paper.
2. In a small saucepan over medium heat, melt 2 ounces butter with brown sugar. Cook for 1 to 2 minutes, or until butter melts and mixture is smooth; pour into prepared pan. Arrange pears, overlapping slightly, over mixture; sprinkle with raisins. Melt remaining 2 ounces butter; set aside.
3. In a medium bowl, whisk together flour, baking soda, cinnamon, ginger, cloves and nutmeg.
4. In a separate medium bowl, whisk together egg and melted butter; whisk in brown sugar, treacle or corn syrup and milk. Stir into flour mixture until blended; spoon mixture over pears.
5. Bake for 35 to 40 minutes, or until a skewer inserted into center comes out clean. Remove from oven; let cool for 15 minutes in pan. Invert cake onto a large plate or platter.
6. To serve, cut cake into slices, dust with confectioners' sugar; serve warm with cream.

Gingerbread Cake

Serves 10 to 12

GINGERBREAD men, gingerbread houses, even the smell of ginger signals Christmas is upon us. Made from sugars and spices brought back from the Middle East by soldiers returning from the Crusades, gingerbread first appeared in central Europe in the Middle Ages. Monks baked gingerbread for religious celebrations, and the first gingerbread man is said to have originated in the court of Queen Elizabeth I who gave important visitors portraits made of ginger-flavored dough. During the nineteenth century, this sweet and spicy cake, generally made with treacle (molasses), became primarily associated with Christmas. This beautiful cake can be served "as is" with a dollop of whipped cream or cut into cubes and used as the base of an old-fashioned trifle. For a festive touch, garnish the cake with Sugared Cranberries and Rosemary (page 96).

- 6 ounces unsalted butter, at room temperature
- 1½ cups (packed) dark brown sugar
- 2 large eggs
- ½ cup molasses
- 2½ cups flour
- 2½ teaspoons ground ginger
- 1 teaspoon ground nutmeg
- ½ teaspoon ground cloves
- 1½ teaspoons cinnamon
- ½ teaspoon allspice
- 1 teaspoon baking powder
- ½ teaspoon salt
- ¼ teaspoon baking soda
- 1 cup water
- Confectioners' sugar, for dusting

1. Preheat oven to 350°F. Coat a 10-inch Bundt pan with baking spray with flour.
2. In the bowl of a stand mixer fitted with the paddle attachment (or with a hand mixer), beat butter and sugar on medium speed until light and fluffy. Add eggs, one at a time, beating well after each addition; beat in molasses.
3. In a large bowl, whisk together flour, ginger, nutmeg, cloves, cinnamon, allspice, baking powder, salt, and baking soda. Add flour mixture to butter mixture in three additions, alternating with water; mix until combined. Transfer to prepared pan.
4. Bake for 55 to 60 minutes, or until a skewer inserted into center comes out clean. Let cool on a wire rack for 10 minutes; loosen cake from pan and invert onto rack. Let cool completely.

Orange Spice Cake

Serves 8

THIS cake is a lovely alternative to the traditional fruit-filled Christmas cake yet it maintains all the festive flavors of holiday fruits and spices. The recipe comes from Helen and Brian Heaton, the brilliant hosts at Castlewood House in Dingle, County Kerry. They suggest you use a thin-skinned seedless orange for the cake rather than any thick-skinned varieties such as Jaffa or Navel as their skin can be bitter.

Cake

- 1 small thin-skinned orange
- 2½ cups self-rising flour
- 3 teaspoons baking powder
- 1 teaspoon ground cinnamon
- 1 teaspoon Mixed Spice (page 92) or pumpkin pie spice
- 1¼ cups sugar
- 8 ounces butter, at room temperature
- 4 large eggs

Filling

- 4 ounces butter, at room temperature
- 4 cups confectioners' sugar
- 2 tablespoons reserved orange pulp
- Orange peel or zest, for garnish

1. Preheat oven to 350°F. Coat two 8-inch baking pans with baking spray with flour; line with a round of parchment paper.
2. Put the orange into a small saucepan; cover with water. Bring to a boil; reduce heat and simmer for about 20 minutes, or until the orange is tender when pierced with tip of a sharp knife. Remove from heat, drain; let cool for about 30 minutes. Cut in half.
3. In a small bowl, sift together flour, baking powder, cinnamon, and Mixed Spice or pumpkin pie spice.
4. Transfer orange halves, including skin, to a food processor; pulse 8 to 10 times, or until chunky. Reserve 2 tablespoons of orange pulp for icing. Return bowl to processor; add flour mixture, sugar, butter, and eggs; process for 20 to 30 seconds, or until mixture is blended (avoid overmixing). Divide mixture evenly between prepared pans.
5. Bake for 25 to 30 minutes, or until a skewer inserted into center comes out clean. Remove from oven; let cool for 5 minutes on wire rack. Invert pans onto rack, peel off wax paper. Let cool completely. Cut each cake in half horizontally to create four layers (see NOTE).
6. Make filling. In bowl of a stand mixer fitted with the paddle attachment (or with a hand mixer), beat butter until smooth. Slowly beat in sugar and reserved orange pulp. With an offset spatula, spread filling between layers and over top of cake. Garnish with orange peel.

NOTE: To cut each layer in half evenly, place toothpicks at the halfway point around the edges of the cake. With a large, serrated knife, slice through cake along toothpick line, slicing slowly to maintain accuracy.

Ingrid Balabanova.

PANETTONE BREAD PUDDING WITH RUM SAUCE

Serves 8

EVEN devoted Irish cooks have discovered panettone, a rich Italian Christmas cake that's sold in markets and specialty stores throughout the festive season. The cake, which comes from the northern Italian city of Milan and whose name translates to "big loaf," is a large, dome-shaped cake that's been leavened with yeast. Light and airy in texture, rich and buttery in taste, the not-too-sweet cake is studded with dried fruits like the ones found in an Irish fruit cake. Grab one to use in this traditional bread and butter pudding laced with lemon curd, or to make an impressive ice cream bombe (page 107). Make the rum sauce while the puddings are baking.

PUDDING

- 1 (2-pound) panettone
- 4 ounces butter, at room temperature
- 8 tablespoons lemon curd
- 5 large eggs
- 2 cups heavy (whipping) cream
- 1 cup sugar

RUM SAUCE

- 2 ounces butter
- 2 tablespoons (packed) dark brown sugar
- 6 tablespoons granulated sugar
- 3 tablespoons dark rum
- 1 cinnamon stick
- 2 tablespoons heavy (whipping) cream

1. Make puddings. Preheat oven to 325°F. Coat eight 6-ounce ramekins with butter flavor cooking spray.
2. Cut panettone into eight 1-inch-thick slices (reserve remaining bread for another use). Spread each slice with 1 tablespoon butter; spread with lemon curd. Cut each slice into squares; loosely fit squares into ramekins.
3. In a large bowl, whisk together eggs, cream, and sugar. Spoon mixture over panettone; press down gently. Let puddings rest for 5 to 10 minutes; spoon any remaining egg mixture over to assure bread is soaked.
4. Bake for 30 minutes, or until puddings rise and tops are lightly browned. Let cool on a wire rack for about 5 minutes. Run a knife around edge of ramekins to loosen; transfer to serving plates. Serve with rum sauce.
5. Make rum sauce. In a medium saucepan, melt butter; stir in brown and granulated sugars. Add rum, cinnamon stick, and cream; bring slowly to a boil. Reduce heat; simmer for 4 to 5 minutes, or until sauce is smooth. Remove from heat; let cool slightly. Just before serving, remove and discard cinnamon stick.

Chocolate Yule Log

Serves 12 to 14

Ayule log is one of the world's most iconic holiday sweets. Widely known as *Bûche de Noël*, French for "Christmas log," the name comes from the ancient practice of burning logs during the Christmas season to protect the house and ward off evil spirits. The origin of the pastry is also linked to the winter solstice festival and the ancient Celtic tradition of burning a log, hoping that its light would entice the sun to return soon. The yule log was a large tree meant to be burned for twelve days in the hearth. The Celts believe the sun stood still during winter solstice, so keeping the yule log burning for these twelve days encouraged the sun to move, making the days longer. As the name suggests, the cake—a chocolate sponge rolled and filled with butter cream and covered with ganache—is made to resemble a log and is usually decorated with festive toppings.

Sponge

- 4 large eggs, at room temperature
- ¾ cup sugar
- 1 teaspoon vanilla bean paste
- ¾ cup flour
- ⅓ cup Dutch-process cocoa powder, plus more for dusting
- 1 teaspoon baking powder
- ½ teaspoon salt
- ⅓ cup sour cream
- ¼ cup canola oil

Filling

- 2½ cups heavy (whipping) cream
- 8 ounces mascarpone cheese
- 1 cup confectioners' sugar
- 2 tablespoons hazelnut liqueur, such as Frangelico
- ½ cup hazelnuts, finely chopped

Ganache

- 1 cup chopped semisweet chocolate
- ¾ cup heavy (whipping) cream
- Pinch of salt
- 1 teaspoon vanilla extract
- 3 ounces unsalted butter, cut into cubes, at room temperature

- ½ cup ground pistachios, for decorating (optional)
- Sugared cranberries and rosemary, for decorating (page 96), optional
- Confectioners' sugar, for dusting

1. Make sponge. Preheat oven to 350°F. Coat a 17x12-inch rimmed baking sheet with baking spray with flour. Line pan with parchment paper; spray parchment. Generously dust a tea towel with cocoa.
2. In the bowl of a stand mixer fitted with the whisk attachment (or with a hand mixer), beat eggs and sugar at medium-high speed for 5 to 7 minutes, or until pale and thick; beat in vanilla bean paste.
3. In a medium bowl, sift together flour, cocoa, baking powder and salt. Gently fold flour mixture into egg mixture in three additions.
4. In a small bowl, whisk together sour cream and oil; fold into egg mixture. With an offset spatula, spread mixture into prepared pan, smoothing top and making sure batter reaches corners.

5. Bake for 10 to 12 minutes, or until top springs back when touched. Turn cake out onto prepared tea towel; gently peel off parchment. Starting with far end, carefully roll up cake with tea towel; let cool on a wire rack.

6. Make filling. In bowl of a stand mixer fitted with the whisk attachment (or with a hand mixer), beat cream, mascarpone, confectioners' sugar and liqueur on medium speed for 5 to 7 minutes, or until stiff peaks form. Carefully unroll cake. Spread filling all over cake, leaving a 1-inch border along edges; sprinkle with hazelnuts. Using tea towel to guide you, slowly reroll cake back up (without towel in between). Wrap in plastic; refrigerate for at least 30 minutes, or overnight, to firm.

7. Make ganache. Put chocolate in a medium bowl. In a small saucepan over medium heat, heat cream. Pour cream over chocolate, let sit for 2 to 3 minutes. Stir until chocolate is melted and smooth. Let cool to room temperature. Beat cooled chocolate with an electric mixer on low speed, adding cubes of butter in three additions. Increase speed to medium; beat until smooth.

8. Remove cake from refrigerator; unwrap. Transfer to a serving platter; trim ends. Cut 2 to 3 inches diagonally from 1 end; place alongside of cake at an angle to create a branch. Attach with ganache. Cut a ¾-inch-thick slice from same end; set on top of cake to create another branch. Attach with ganache. Spread remaining filling all over outside of cake. Use an offset spatula and drag along cake to create bark ridges or score with a skewer or fork to create thinner bark. Decorate with sugared cranberries and rosemary; sprinkle ground pistachios around bottom of cake to resemble moss, if desired.

9. To serve, sprinkle with confectioners' sugar before cutting log into slices.

CHRISTMAS ICE CREAM BOMBE

Serves 8

THIS impressive dessert uses Italian panettone, a popular and widely accessible Christmas fruit bread, to create an ice cream "bombe" (also known as bombe glacée in French). It's a round dessert with an ice cream center, and in this recipe it's surrounded by the panettone. Depending on the size of your pudding bowl, you might have a few slices of bread left over. No worries; panettone makes delicious French toast. If you want to completely coat the bombe, double the amount of both the dark and white chocolate.

- 1 (2-pound) panettone
- 1½ quarts vanilla ice cream, softened
- 4 ounces dark chocolate
- 2 ounces white chocolate
- ¼ cup flaked almonds
- ¼ cup chopped pistachios
- ¼ cup dried cranberries
- Sugared rosemary (page 96), for garnish (optional)

1. Line a medium freezer safe bowl with plastic wrap leaving a 6-inch overhang (to cover ice cream when assembled).
2. Slice off top dome of panettone (cut down to paper wrapping); remove paper. Place top, rounded-side down, in prepared bowl. Cut off a 1-inch-thick slice from bottom; reserve.
3. Slice rest of loaf horizontally into 1-inch-thick slices; cut each slice in half. Stand panettone halves around sides of bowl, overlapping slightly to fully line bowl (cut small wedges, if necessary, to fill in gaps.)
4. Spoon softened ice cream into bowl, pressing firmly to create a level base. Put reserved bottom slice on top of ice cream; fold plastic wrap over. Freeze for at least 2 hours or overnight.
5. In a microwave-safe bowl, melt dark chocolate. In a separate microwave-safe bowl, melt white chocolate.
6. To serve, remove bomb from freezer. Uncover plastic wrap from top of bombe. Invert onto a serving plate; unwrap remaining plastic wrap. Pour dark chocolate over bombe; drizzle white chocolate over dark. Sprinkle with almonds, pistachios, and cranberries; garnish with sugared rosemary, if desired. Return to freezer until serving time.
7. To serve, run a knife under hot water and cut bombe into slices.

Isabel Poulin

HOLIDAY TRADITIONS

CAKES, FRUITCAKES, AND BEADS

Many Irish traditions stem from Celtic mythology and Christian rituals. The tradition of feasting on Christmas Day marks the end of Advent, a four-week period of fasting in the Christian calendar. The Christmas cakes, fruitcakes, and special breads savored on that day have always held a special place in the Celtic household. Mince pies and plum puddings were symbols of a fertile and rich reserve from which new energy would emerge.

BAUBLES FOR THE TREE

The earliest Christmas tree decorations were fruits and nuts; later paper streamers and bits of shiny metal or foil were used. In German households, gingerbread, hard cookies, lace, and cut outs from magazine illustrations became popular baubles followed by colorful glass ornaments hand-blown by German artisans.

THE LADEN TABLE

After the evening meal on Christmas Eve, the kitchen table was set again. Families placed a loaf of bread filled with caraway seeds and raisins and a pitcher of milk on it, lit a large candle, and left the door to the house unlatched so that Mary and Joseph, or any wandering traveler, could be welcomed. Hospitality is a way of life in Ireland, and anyone who visits the house is entertained with tea and cakes, especially during the holidays.

St. Mary's Church, Cockhill, Co. Donegal | *Donal Kearney*

CHAPTER FIVE

YULETIDE

THE TWELVE DAYS OF CHRISTMAS

And it was always said of him that he knew how to keep Christmas well,
If any man alive possessed the knowledge. May that be truly said of us, and all of us!
And so, as Tiny Tim observed, God bless us everyone.
CHARLES DICKENS, *A CHRISTMAS CAROL*

Wren Day Festivities, Dingle, Co. Kerry | *Gerald Horgan*

ST. STEPHEN'S DAY/BOXING DAY/HUNTING THE WREN

In Christian theology, Advent is the four-week season of fasting leading up to the celebration of Christmas. On the other side of Christmas is Twelvetide, or Yuletide, the twelve-day festive season that marks the span between the birth of Christ on December 25 (the first day) and the coming of the Magi on January 6 (the twelfth day).

For many, things go back to business-as-usual once Christmas Day is over, but in Ireland (and other countries including the United Kingdom and its former colonies) the sacred and secular converge with days that are celebrated as both national and religious holidays. St. Stephen's Day, for example, celebrated on December 26, is a feast day as well as a national holiday in the Republic of Ireland. In Northern Ireland, which is part of the United Kingdom, it's a national holiday known as Boxing Day, a term first recorded in 1833. It's a tradition that some say stems from a time when servants, who waited on their masters all year, were given the day off and treated to boxes filled with gifts, money, or Christmas leftovers in appreciation of their service. In the Victorian era, it became a tradition for clergy to encourage donations to the poor. They placed collection boxes in churches on Christmas day and distributed the alms on the next day, one that came to be known as "Boxing Day."

One of the richest traditions observed in some parts of the Republic of Ireland is the age-old custom of "Hunting the Wren," an event that also takes place on St. Stephen's Day. The festival, known as *lá an Dreolín* in Irish, commemorates an ancient ritual of rural revelers who would travel from door to door begging for money or treats. The participants, originally called Wren Boys or mummers, often carried a wren (sometimes pronounced and written "wran") in a cage and pretended that the bird was asking for alms. More popular, however, was the tradition of carrying a stuffed wren hung on a pole or placed in a bed of evergreens or furze, a spiny shrub. As they walked around the village, they sang: "The wren, the wren, the king of all birds, St. Stephen's Day was caught in the furze; Up with kattle and down with the pan, Give us our hansel [money] to bury the wren."

The Wren Boys came masked and dressed in outlandish costumes or motley clothing, often made of straw. They would visit houses in rural neighborhoods, playing accordions and drums called bodhráns (pronounced "bow-rawn") and begging for donations for the evening's Wren dance. Tradition has it that the first group of Wren Boys would be welcomed to a house because they were said to bring good luck, but those who came afterwards were usually not as well appreciated. At the end of the day, it was customary to bury the wren, so if the boys weren't suitably rewarded at a particular household, they retaliated by burying the wren opposite the front door to prevent luck from entering the house for that year.

Although this tradition has died out in many parts of Ireland, it's very much alive in Dingle, County Kerry. In his book *Green and Gold: The Wrenboys of Dingle*, local author Steve MacDonogh wrote: "The Wren is an explosion of light, color, and boisterous exuberance in the midst of winter's gloom and has continued as an unbroken tradition—changing, but never dying out." The great tradition in Dingle is quite competitive, with Wren Boys from the main Wren groups of the town vying for bragging rights for "best turn-out," "best music," and "best rigs."

Kerrygold

PLOUGHMAN'S LUNCH WITH PEAR AND CRANBERRY CHUTNEY

Serves 6 to 8

For most folks, December 26 is a lazy day to relax, to watch a sporting event like hurling, rugby, football or horse racing, or to gather again with family or friends who weren't seen on Christmas Day; it's also a popular shopping holiday. There's no holiday from food, though, and while individual families have their own food traditions for the day—many simply repeat the entire Christmas meal and serve it buffet style—the most universal tradition involves using leftovers in as many recipes as possible and to prepare quick-to-reheat dishes in advance. A dish that involves no cooking, however, and one that makes the most of leftover meat and cheese from the Christmas feast, is a ploughman's lunch, a popular dish in Irish pubs and restaurants. It's beyond perfect for a December 26 lunch and one of the easiest meals to assemble, yes, assemble, because that's about all you have to do to bring it to the table. The traditional salad is made with sliced meats—most often turkey, ham, or roast beef—and it can easily be served buffet style to cater to a crowd. It's open to wide interpretation, but always includes slices of cheese, a bit of salad, crusty French bread or slices of brown soda bread, and a ramekin filled with chutney. You can add smoked salmon or trout if you have it. Serve it with this make-ahead Pear and Cranberry Chutney, with Pear and Apple Chutney (page 23), or with one of the cranberry sauces on page 79. Drizzle with your favorite vinaigrette.

PEAR AND CRANBERRY CHUTNEY

- ◦ 1 tablespoon canola oil
- ◦ 1 medium onion, chopped
- ◦ 3 firm ripe pears, peeled, cored, and chopped
- ◦ ¾ cup dried cranberries
- ◦ ½ cup (packed) light brown sugar
- ◦ 4 tablespoons cider vinegar
- ◦ 1 tablespoon grated fresh ginger
- ◦ ½ teaspoon ground cinnamon
- ◦ ¼ teaspoon ground cloves
- ◦ Pinch of cayenne pepper

SALAD

- ◦ 6 to 8 slices Cheddar cheese
- ◦ 6 to 8 slices Swiss cheese
- ◦ 6 to 8 slices blue cheese
- ◦ 6 to 8 slices ham
- ◦ 6 to 8 slices roast beef
- ◦ 6 to 8 slices turkey
- ◦ 4 to 6 ounces smoked trout (optional)
- ◦ 4 to 6 ounces smoked salmon (optional)
- ◦ Salad greens, tomatoes, cucumbers, for serving
- ◦ Wholegrain mustard, for serving
- ◦ Bread, for serving
- ◦ Vinaigrette, for drizzling

1. Make chutney. In medium saucepan over medium heat, heat oil. Add onion; cook, stirring frequently, for 3 to 5 minutes, or until soft but not browned. Add pears, cranberries, brown sugar, vinegar, ginger, cinnamon, cloves, and pepper. Bring to a boil. Reduce heat to medium-low; cook, stirring frequently, for about 30 minutes, or until pears are soft and most of the liquid has evaporated.
2. Remove from heat; let cool completely. (Cover and refrigerate for up to 2 weeks). Serve at room temperature.
3. Make salad. On a large decorative platter, arrange the cheeses, meats, poultry, and fish (if using).
4. Arrange salad greens, tomatoes, and cucumbers (if using). Serve with mustard, chutney, and bread. Drizzle with vinaigrette or serve alongside.

TURKEY AND HAM PIE

Serve 6 to 8

LEFTOVER ham and cheese from the Christmas meal will never go to waste when you combine them in a delicious pot pie that could easily be named "St. Stephen's Day Pie" given its popularity on post-Christmas menus. A chef-friend offered it to me several years ago and suggests that cranberry sauce or chutney (page 79, 115) is the perfect accompaniment.

- 3 ounces butter
- 2 small onions, chopped
- 4 ounces button mushroom, sliced
- ⅓ cup flour
- 3¼ cups turkey stock or canned low-sodium chicken broth
- 1 tablespoon Dijon mustard
- 1½ teaspoons chopped fresh tarragon
- 1½ cups diced cooked turkey
- 1½ cups diced cooked ham
- 1 cup diced cooked carrots
- 1 cup frozen peas
- 2 tablespoons chopped fresh flatleaf parsley
- Ground black pepper
- 1 sheet frozen puff pastry, thawed according to package directions
- 1 large egg mixed with 1 tablespoon water, for egg wash

1. Preheat oven to 375°F. Coat a 2-quart baking dish with butter flavor cooking spray.
2. In a large skillet over medium heat, melt butter. Add onions; cook for 3 to 5 minutes, or until soft but not browned. Add mushrooms; cook for 2 minutes. Whisk in flour; cook and stir for 3 minutes, or until blended. Stir in stock or broth; bring to a boil. Cook for 3 to 5 minutes, or until mixture thickens.
3. Stir in mustard, tarragon, turkey, ham, carrots, peas, and parsley; season with pepper. Spoon mixture into prepared dish.
4. Unfold the pastry; roll gently to remove creases. Place pastry on top of mixture; trim excess. Press pastry to the rim to seal; cut a few slits on top to release steam. Brush with egg wash.
5. Bake for 25 minutes, or until mixture is bubbling and pastry is golden. Serve immediately.

Ham, Cheese, and Mushroom Quiche

Serves 6 to 8

ANOTHER tasty recipe for leftover ham and cheese is this quiche—served hot or at room temperature —that's perfect for breakfast, brunch, or on a post-Christmas buffet. Use a refrigerated pie crust for the bottom of the quiche or bake it without a crust for the same delicious flavor.

- 1 refrigerated pie crust (optional)
- 2 ounces butter
- 1 small shallot, minced
- 2 ounces wild mushrooms, chopped
- 2 tablespoons Dijon mustard, divided
- 1 cup chopped cooked ham
- 4 ounces shredded Swiss cheese
- 4 large eggs
- 1 cup heavy (whipping) cream
- Ground black pepper

1. Preheat oven to 375°F. Slowly unroll crust (if using); place in an ungreased 9-inch glass pie dish. Press firmly against sides and bottom. Fold crust under and press together to form thick crust edge; flute edges (do not prick bottom or sides of crust). Bake for 10 to 12 minutes, or until lightly browned; let cool on a wire rack.
2. In a small skillet over medium heat, melt butter. Cook shallots and mushrooms for 3 to 5 minutes, or until soft but not browned.
3. Brush 1 tablespoon mustard over bottom of crust to seal; sprinkle ham over crust. Spread mushroom mixture over ham; sprinkle with cheese.
4. In a medium bowl, whisk together eggs, cream, remaining mustard and pepper; pour over crust. Place dish on a baking sheet
5. Bake for 30 to 35 minutes, or until filling is set (if edge of crust browns too quickly, cover with foil or pie crust shield after 15 minutes to prevent excessive browning). Remove from oven; let cool for 15 minutes before cutting into slices. Serve warm or at room temperature.

Ham, Swiss, and Mushroom Strata

Serves 8 to 10

For this delicious post-Christmas dish, use Emmental, Gruyère, or Jarlsburg cheese, all Swiss-style in appearance with a mild, buttery and nutty taste. While these cheeses originated in countries outside of Ireland, Kerrygold produces its own version of both Swiss and Emmental, and Dairygold produces Jarlsburg for a Norwegian cheesemaking company at its dairy co-op in Mogeely, County Cork. For best results, refrigerate the strata (the name means "layers") for at least two hours or overnight

- 4 tablespoons extra virgin olive oil, divided
- 2 large shallots, finely chopped
- 4 Portobello mushroom caps
- 1 ounce unsalted butter
- ½ cup chopped flat-leaf parsley
- 1 loaf brioche, challah or French bread, cut into 1-inch pieces
- 10 ounces Emmental, Gruyère or Jarlsburg cheese, cut into ½-inch pieces
- 6 large eggs
- 3 cups milk
- ½ cup heavy cream
- 1 teaspoon salt
- ¼ teaspoon ground black pepper

1. In a large skillet over medium heat, heat 2 tablespoons oil. Add shallots; cook for 5 minutes, or until softened but not browned. Transfer shallots to a medium bowl.
2. Cut mushroom caps in half; slice halves into ¼-inch-thick slices. Return skillet to medium heat; melt butter. Add mushrooms; cook, stirring frequently, for about 10 minutes, or until softened and browned. Transfer mushrooms to bowl with shallots; stir in parsley.
3. Coat a 13x9-inch baking dish with nonstick cooking spray. Place half of bread cubes in dish; top with two thirds of mushroom mixture. Sprinkle with two thirds of cheese. Cover with remaining bread, mushroom mixture and cheese.
4. In a large bowl, whisk together eggs, milk, cream, salt and pepper.
5. Pour evenly over strata, making sure to moisten all bread cubes on top. Wrap securely with plastic wrap; refrigerate at least 2 hours or overnight.
6. Preheat oven to 325°F. Bake strata, uncovered, for 75 minutes, or until golden brown and puffed. (Check strata after 60 minutes; if top is getting too browned, cover dish loosely with foil.) Remove from oven; let cool a wire rack for 5 minutes before cutting into squares. Serve warm.

MINCEMEAT AND APPLE PUDDING WITH CUSTARD SAUCE

Serves 10

ANYONE who loves mincemeat can never have too many recipes for ways to use it beyond the traditional tart or pie. The fruity mix goes especially well with tart apples in this pudding, a delicious cakelike-sweet. (The pudding can be made 1 to 2 days in advance and reheated). Top it with Custard Sauce or Brandy Butter (page 89).

PUDDING

- 2 Granny Smith apples, peeled, cored, and chopped
- 2 tablespoons light brown sugar
- Grated zest and juice of 1 lemon
- 5 ounces butter, at room temperature
- ⅔ cup granulated sugar
- 3 large eggs
- ⅓ cup plus 1 tablespoon homemade or prepared mincemeat
- 1 teaspoon vanilla extract
- 1¼ cups flour
- 1½ teaspoons baking powder
- ¼ teaspoon salt
- 1 teaspoon ground cinnamon
- ½ teaspoon ground nutmeg
- 1 tablespoon milk

CUSTARD SAUCE

- 2¼ cups milk
- ¼ cup heavy (whipping) cream
- 2 teaspoons vanilla bean paste
- 5 large egg yolks
- 2 tablespoons sugar
- 2 teaspoons corn starch

1. Make pudding. Preheat oven to 325°F. Coat a 9-inch springform pan with butter flavor cooking spray.
2. In a large bowl, toss apples with brown sugar, lemon zest, and juice; spread evenly into bottom of prepared pan.
3. In the bowl of a stand mixer fitted with the paddle attachment (or with a hand mixer), beat butter and sugar on medium speed until light and fluffy. Beat in eggs, one at a time, beating well after each addition. Stir in vanilla and mincemeat.
4. In a medium bowl, whisk together flour, baking powder, salt, cinnamon, and nutmeg. Stir into mincemeat mixture; stir in milk. Spoon mixture over apples; smooth top.
5. Bake for 45 to 50 minutes, or until top is golden and springs back when lightly touched. Serve warm or at room temperature with custard sauce.
6. Make custard sauce. In a medium saucepan over medium-low heat, bring milk and cream to simmer; stir occasionally. Stir in vanilla bean paste.
7. In a medium saucepan over medium heat, whisk together egg yolks, sugar, and corn starch; bring gently to simmer. Slowly pour into cream mixture, whisking constantly until blended. Return pan to heat; continue to whisk until thick and smooth. Serve warm, or at room temperature. (If not serving immediately, transfer custard to a bowl and press a piece of plastic wrap directly on surface to prevent a skin from forming).

Bartosz Luczak

MINCEMEAT CAKE WITH LEMON CURD CREAM

Serves 10 to 12

THIS mincemeat cake is perfect "as is," or if you cut it into cubes it's a lovely alternative to pound cake or ladyfingers as the basis of a holiday trifle. Substitute the lemon curd whipped cream for traditional custard and sprinkle colorful pomegranate arils in between the layers. This make-ahead sweet is perfect for a post-Christmas buffet or to serve at teatime.

CAKE

- 6 ounces butter, at room temperature
- ½ cup sugar
- 2 large eggs
- ½ teaspoon vanilla extract
- 1¾ cups flour
- 1½ teaspoons baking powder
- ½ teaspoon baking soda
- ¼ teaspoon salt
- ⅓ cup milk
- 1 cup homemade or prepared mincemeat

LEMON CURD CREAM

- 2 cups heavy (whipping) cream
- 5 tablespoons lemon curd
- Grated zest of 1 lemon
- 6 tablespoons confectioners' sugar

- Pomegranate arils (optional)

1. Make cake. Preheat oven to 350° F. Coat a 9-inch loaf pan with baking spray with flour.
2. In the bowl of a stand mixer fitted with the paddle attachment (or with a hand mixer), beat butter and sugar on medium speed until light and fluffy. Beat in eggs, one at a time, beating well after each addition; add vanilla.
3. In a large bowl, whisk together flour, baking powder, baking soda, and salt. Beat in flour mixture in three additions, alternating with milk; fold in mincemeat. Transfer to prepared pan.
4. Bake for 45 to 50 minutes, or until a skewer inserted into center comes out clean. Let cool on a wire rack for 25 minutes. Loosen cake from pan; invert onto rack. Let cool completely.
5. Make lemon curd cream. In the bowl of a stand mixer fitted with the whisk (or with a hand mixer), whip cream, lemon curd and zest on medium-high speed until soft peaks form; gradually add confectioners' sugar. Continue to beat until stiff peaks form.
6. If making a trifle, cut cake into 1-inch cubes. Layer about one-third cake cubes in a 4-quart trifle bowl (or use a deep glass bowl). Spoon some lemon curd cream on top; sprinkle with some pomegranate arils. Repeat layers twice. Spread whipped cream on top; sprinkle with additional arils and garnish with sugared cranberries and rosemary, if desired. Serve immediately, or cover and refrigerate for up to 24 hours.

CRANBERRY AND CASHEL BLUE TART

Serves 8 to 10

STILTON, one of the world's most well-known names in blue cheese, has been called "the king of every Christmas cheeseboard." But that was before 1984 when Louis and Jane Grubb started to produce Cashel Blue, Ireland's first farmhouse blue cheese, at their Beechmount Farm in Fethard, County Tipperary. It now takes pride of place on an Irish cheeseboard and is a lovely ingredient in this savory tart enhanced with the festive addition of cranberries. Perfect for any holiday event, from Christmas Eve to a Woman's Christmas tea, you can make it as one large tart and cut it into slices or serve it as tartlets.

- 1 refrigerated pie crust, at room temperature
- 8 ounces cream cheese, at room temperature
- 3 ounces crumbled Cashel Blue cheese, at room temperature
- 2 tablespoon milk
- 1 large egg, beaten
- ¾ cup fresh or frozen cranberries
- 2 tablespoon chopped chives
- Ground black pepper
- 2 tablespoons chopped walnuts

1. Preheat oven to 450°F. Slowly unroll pie crust and place in an ungreased 9-inch tart pan with removable bottom. Press firmly against side and bottom. Fold excess crust under and press together to form a thick crust edge; flute edges. Prick bottom and side with a fork. Bake for about 10 minutes, or until lightly browned. Cool 10 minutes; reduce oven temperature to 375°F.
2. In a medium bowl, beat cream cheese and blue cheese with an electric mixer on medium speed until blended; beat in milk and egg until smooth. Stir in cranberries, chives, and pepper. Sprinkle walnuts over crust; spread cheese mixture on top.
3. Bake for 20 to 25 minutes, or until filling is set. Remove from oven; let cool for 30 minutes before cutting into slices. (Can be made 1 day ahead; cover and refrigerate).

Merrion Hotel, Dublin

NOLLAIG NA MBAN

The twelfth day of Christmas, January 6, officially marks the end of the Christmas season in Ireland. It's also one of the most important days on the calendar after Christmas Day itself, celebrated as the Christian Feast of the Epiphany when the Three Kings arrived in Bethlehem with their offerings to the newly born Christ. It's also a traditional celebration known as *Nollaig na mBan* (Women's Christmas), a day when Irish women who had worked tirelessly for weeks to create Christmas magic for their families had the day completely to themselves.

In rural Ireland, in the days when women would have raised a few turkeys for sale at Christmas markets, they would have kept the money to spend exclusively on themselves at the end of the season. The men of the house would take over the running of the house for the day, cleaning, preparing meals, and looking after the children. This left the woman of the house free to socialize with female relatives and friends after a busy and exhausting holiday season, to gather for afternoon tea, and, more importantly, to take the day off.

Irish folklore scholar Kevin Danaher mentioned the date in his 1970s book *The Year In Ireland: A Calendar*, when he suggested that the name "Women's Christmas" is explained by "the assertion that Christmas Day was marked by beef, whiskey and men's fare, while on Little Christmas Day the dainties preferred by women—cake, tea and wine—were more in evidence." It became a day for women "to go visiting in the afternoon, eat a slice of currant loaf, have a cup of tea, a chat and to rest."

Over time, many *Nollaig na mBan* customs faded away, except in *Gaeltacht* (Irish-speaking) areas of Cork, Kerry, and the west of Ireland. It's been suggested that the slow demise of the Irish language has contributed to the fading of this custom with its Gaelic name, but in recent years, the tradition has been revived a bit. In modern Ireland, where housework is generally more equitably divided, the day has shifted somewhat to being a celebration and acknowledgment of women, and many women's groups mark the day with charitable events or donations to organizations that support women's causes. Many restaurants, hotels, and bars around the country host *Nollaig na mBan* celebrations such as afternoon tea—with a bit of bubbly, of course!

In many Irish homes, January 6 is also the day when Christmas decorations are packed up and stored away for another year. When holly and ivy were the traditional decorations in Irish homes, they were taken down and burnt on the twelfth day, and even today many Irish people will tell you it's bad luck to have your decorations up beyond January 6. At the end of the eighteenth and nineteenth centuries, Twelfth Night was an important day in the Christian calendar and parties were held to celebrate—perhaps, a precursor to modern-day festivities.

Brian Morrison

FOR MORE INFORMATION ABOUT
Margaret M. Johnson
&
Festive Flavors of Ireland
please visit:

www.irishcook.com
www.facebook.com/IrishCookbook

For more information about
AMBASSADOR INTERNATIONAL
please visit:

www.ambassador-international.com
@AmbassadorIntl
www.facebook.com/AmbassadorIntl

Made in the USA
Middletown, DE
15 November 2021